P. 99

The World's
MOST
INFAMOUS
MURDERS

The World's MOST INFAMOUS MURDERS

**Roger Boar
&
Nigel Blundell**

Contents

Acknowledgements

The authors wish to thank the following for research, suggestions and contributions in the preparation of this book: Fred Wehner, Martin Dunn, Robin Corry, Rob Robbins, Jitka Markova, Don Mackay, John Beattie, Susan Marchant, Kendal McDonald, Frederic Rolph and Stella Duggan.

The publishers would like to thank the following individuals and organizations for their kind permission to reproduce the photographs in this book:

Associated Press 2 above left, 59, 63, Mary Evans Picture Library 140, Popperfoto Limited 9, 67, Radio Times Hulton Picture Library 2 below right, 3, 25, 55, 103, 109, 139, 143, 177, Syndication International 2 above right, 13, 27, 41, 51, 55, inset, 85, 120, 124, 169 below right, 172, John Topham Picture Library 2 below left, 18, 40, 45, 64, 93, 94, 95, 123, 129, 133, 145, 151, 155 163, 165, 166, 169, 171, 185, 191.

First published in hardback in 1983
by Octopus Books Limited
59 Grosvenor Street
London W1

Paperback edition first published in 1984

© Octopus Books Limited

ISBN 0 7064 2148 5

Made and printed in Great Britain by
Richard Clay (The Chaucer Press) Limited
Bungay, Suffolk

Introduction

Life is very frail, death very final and murder often a simple crime to commit. Which is perhaps why that fearful crime so fascinates us all.

Most people at one time or another have thought or said: I'd like to murder him. Or her. They do not usually mean it, but the thought is there.

Most murders are not committed with premeditation. They are the product of one manic moment. Often they are the result of long pent-up emotions erupting in a fatal outburst when the mind can take no more and restraint suddenly snaps.

But there are other causes of murder; more sinister, less simple to understand, less easy to forgive.

The murders that horrify us most are those caused by greed or envy, or those which are the sadistic product of a twisted mind. Sometimes they seem to be caused by nothing but sheer bloodlust.

Assembled in this volume are the most infamous of those killings. They are collected together in no particular order . . . there is no league table of terror and the awfulness of the crimes defies analysis.

No-one, for instance, can hope to explain the savage slaughters of Jack the Ripper, the maniacal fervour of Charles Manson's band of assassins, the callous child slayings of the Moors Murderers.

The type of crime the reader will find in the following pages is that which Shakespeare described as:

'Murder most foul, as in the best it is;

But this most foul, strange and unnatural.'   *Hamlet*

The Son of Sam

DAVID BERKOWITZ

Son of Sam killer David Berkowitz cold-bloodedly murdered six people and wounded another seven during the year he terrorized New York. He shot five women and one man dead in a series of vicious killings which spread panic round the city during 1977. Son of Sam struck at courting couples and lone women. The killer also turned his gun on two dogs. When the spate of killings were linked, hysteria mounted. Discos and restaurants were deserted as the frightened population made sure they were home before dark.

It was in the last few months Berkowitz was at large that he became known as Son of Sam. Police found a letter lying in the road just a few yards from the dead bodies of two young lovers. The letter read: 'Dear Captain Joseph Borelli, I am deeply hurt by your calling me a woman hater. I am not. But I am a monster. I am the Son of Sam.' Berkowitz left the letter in the road after he fired at a couple as they embraced in a car.

He had already killed three people and wounded four, but after the chilling letter was published New York's Mayor Beame ordered police: 'Catch this man.' A special squad of 200 detectives was formed. Every rumour and tip-off was followed up but the identity of the killer remained a mystery. More than 100 police were put on nightly patrols in areas of the Bronx and Queens where it was thought he might strike again.

Police described the killer as 'neurotic, schizophrenic and paranoid'. They came up with the theory that he might believe himself the victim of demonic possession. Because of the uncanny way Berkowitz escaped detection, it was believed at one time that he might be a policeman using inside information to vanish undetected. Meanwhile the killings continued.

One night a high-school girl and her boyfriend were shot as they got into their car. Berkowitz fired through the windscreen, hitting the boy in the arm and the girl in the head, neck and shoulder. A month later he struck again. Two 20-year-olds on their first date together were shot as they kissed in a car. Bobby Violante was just telling Stacy Moskowitz how much he cared for her when the bullet which was to blind him smashed into his face. Stacy was also shot in the head, and she died 38 hours later on a hospital operating table.

Berkowitz was caught eventually because of a parking ticket. He watched from the shadows while police stuck a ticket on his car. When they had gone he

David Berkowitz with inset of 17-year-old
victim, Judy Placido

walked over and screwed up the ticket. But he was seen by a woman walking her dog. She thought he had a strange smile on his face and when he came close to her she saw he had a gun in his hand. She called the police the next day and told them about the parking ticket. They traced the car through their records. The next day police lay in wait for Berkowitz. He walked to his car with the .44 calibre gun in a paper bag. When challenged he told police in his soft voice: 'I'm Sam.' The officers remember that he had a peculiar, child-like smile on his face. At his trial he claimed bloodthirsty demons made him kill. He said that one of the dogs he shot had the spirit of a 6,000-year-old man who ordered him to kill.

Berkowitz, now 28, was sentenced to 30 years in jail after he pleaded guilty to the series of attacks and killings. Since his trial he has claimed that he was a member of a New York satanic cult and other men were involved in the murders. Now he passes his days writing letters to girlfriends, newspapers, congressmen and journalists.

Police still believe that Berkowitz acted alone. But other people take seriously his claims that more people were involved. Eyewitness descriptions of the killer varied markedly in height and appearance. And none of the four different police sketches of the murderer closely resembled Berkowitz. Nor does the handwriting on many of the messages sent to police and newspapers by Son of Sam match up with Berkowitz's. The most intriguing riddle involves Sam Carr, who owned the dog that Berkowitz claimed bewitched him. Carr's two sons, John and Michael, both died in suspicious circumstances after Berkowitz was arrested. John Carr was found shot to death in his girlfriend's apartment and Michael died when his car crashed for no apparent reason. These factors have led some lawyers to claim that Berkowitz was only a lookout for a group involved in the murder conspiracy.

People who knew Berkowitz before his arrest say he was a loner without any personal charms. He loved to gorge himself on junk food. His favourite meal

> **Mentally deranged sex-maniac, German-born Bruno Ludke, had committed no fewer than 85 murders before his arrest in 1943. From the age of 18 he raped, robbed, stabbed or strangled his prey for pleasure. When humans were not available he resorted to torturing animals. Finally, when Ludke was arrested for sexual assault, Himmler's SS sterilised him. When he confessed to all his crimes, his prosecutors realized that, in several cases, other people had been executed for Ludke's killings. The scandal was hushed up and Ludke was sent to hospital in Vienna, where he became the guinea pig for medical and psychiatric experiments. He died there in 1944.**

was hamburgers followed by chocolate ice-cream. When he was arrested, police at first took him to be retarded. Two guns were pressed against his head and he was ordered to 'freeze', but his only response was to keep smiling. Arresting officer John Falotico remembers: 'He had that stupid smile on his face, like it was a kid's game.'

Nobody knows why Berkowitz started to kill. But after the first killing of Donna Lauria, the murders became an addiction. He drove around New York night after night looking for victims. He also liked to return to the scene of his murders. One night after shooting a courting couple, instead of fleeing the scene he drove on a few blocks to catch a glimpse of the apartment block where his first victim Donna had lived. He told police that after a murder he felt 'flushed with power'. After a killing he would go to a late night snack bar to eat his favourite chocolate desserts.

It was Berkowitz's ordinariness that helped him escape capture. At one place where he lodged, all that the family could remember of him was that he was a 'regular sort of guy who used to take his car out in the middle of the night'.

Since he has been in prison Berkowitz has gone some way to achieving his ambition of becoming a celebrity. He has unlimited letter writing privileges and conducts torrid pen-pal romances with women. Berkowitz has made more than $200,000 from various articles, a book and film rights to his life. A court battle by the relatives of his victims to prevent him getting any of the money failed.

The Glamorous Lovers

BONNIE PARKER AND CLYDE BARROW

Despite the popular image of Bonnie and Clyde as glamorous, rather hard-done-by bank robbers, the reality was very different; they were extremely vicious thieves and murderers.

Handsome Clyde Barrow was born on 24 March 1909 to a poor Texas farmer. Even as a young child he displayed sadistic tendencies, taking great delight in torturing farm animals.

Bonnie Parker born in 1911 came from a devout Baptist family. Her father died when she was four and the family then moved to Cement City, Texas. She was a pretty, petite girl with blue eyes and fair hair. Bonnie had married a Dallas tearaway named Roy Thornton when she was only 16 but the marriage had ended when he was sentenced to 99 years' jail for murder. Her mother was delighted when she met Clyde Barrow because she felt he would help Bonnie to get over her broken marriage. Bonnie was then nineteen-years-old and Clyde twenty-one.

Their relationship did not get off to a good start. The first night that Clyde visited Bonnie's house he was arrested on seven accounts of burglary and car theft. He was given a sentence of two years, but escaped when Bonnie smuggled a gun into the jail. He was recaptured after robbing a railway office at gunpoint, only a few days after his escape. Clyde Barrow was sentenced to prison for fourteen years.

Life in Texas prisons was brutal and extremely tough. Desperate to get out,

---

Charles Arthur Floyd, a strapping farm worker from Okalahoma, felt that he had suffered enough poverty in his life – so he took to robbing banks and machine-gunning guards. A madam of a whorehouse in Kansas City nicknamed him 'Pretty Boy' Floyd and the title stuck to him throughout his criminal career.

During one bank robbery getaway he killed a policeman and was sentenced to 15 years. But he escaped from the train taking him to jail and went on to commit numerous other robberies and at least two more murders. An FBI bullet finally struck him down in a field at East Liverpool, Ohio, in 1934.

Bonnie Parker and Clyde Barrow

> **Blackbeard was the monster of the Spanish Main whose overpowering 2 metre (6ft 4in) frame put the fear of God in both foes and allies.** He had no hesitation in shooting his men – just to let others know who was in charge.
>   Despite his Latin looks, Blackbeard was born Edward Teach in Bristol, England. He fed his sexual appetite with a bevy of 14 wives and mistresses. And when he was in a flirtatious mood, he would adorn his twisted black beard with silk ribbon. When a price of £100 was put on the scoundrel's head, he met his match in Lieutenant Maynard, captain of a British boat. In 1718 Maynard cornered Blackbeard's boat and he and his men fired 25 shots into his body. Maynard celebrated his victory by flying the murderer's beard from the bowsprit.

Clyde persuaded another prisoner to cut off two of his toes with an axe. He was released on crutches and headed straight back to Bonnie.

To please Bonnie's mother he took a job in Massachusetts in an attempt to make an honest living. However, he could not bear being so far from home and was soon back in West Dallas. Bonnie left home just three days later, to embark on a life of robbery and murder. The couple were joined by a friend of Clyde's called Ray Hamilton, and two other men.

The first murder was committed in April 1932 for the paltry sum of $40 when they shot a jeweller named John W. Bucher in Hillsboro, Texas. Bonnie was in jail at the time on suspicion of having stolen a car, but she was released three months later without any charges having been made. During that time Clyde and his associates brutally gunned down a Sheriff and a Deputy-Sheriff outside a dancehall.

The gang's biggest ever haul was $3,500, stolen from a filling station at Grand Prairie. Bonnie and Clyde decided to celebrate with a motoring holiday around Missouri, Kansas and Michigan, staying at top hotels and eating at expensive restaurants.

Not surprisingly, the money did not last long. They reverted to petty crime, murdering for surprisingly small amounts of money. Bonnie coolly shot a Texas butcher three times in the stomach before robbing him, and William Jones, a 16-year-old member of the Barrow gang, shot dead the son of the owner of a car they were caught stealing. Shooting to kill was now an automatic reflex.

In March 1933 the gang was joined in Missouri by Clyde's brother, Buck, and Blanche, Buck's wife. They narrowly escaped arrest from the apartment they were all staying in and shot dead two policemen in their escape bid.

It was now no longer safe for the fugitives to stay anywhere and they fled from town to town, robbing and killing as they went. They were both very aware that they would not remain at liberty for much longer and, indeed, Bonnie predicted their deaths in her poem, *The Story of Bonnie and Clyde*. Their greatest fear seemed to be that they would not see their parents again, to whom they were both deeply attached.

Near Wellington, Texas, their car plunged to the bottom of a gorge. Clyde and Jones were thrown clear but Bonnie was trapped and seriously burned when it caught fire. She was rescued, with the help of a local farmer. The gang were sheltered for a few days by the farmer and his family who soon became suspicious and called the police. Once again, the fugitives escaped at gunpoint, and were rejoined by Buck and Blanche. Bonnie was still seriously ill.

In July the gang decided to rest at a tourist camp in Missouri. Again, the police surrounded them. Although they shot their way to freedom Buck had been hit through the temple and Blanche was blinded by glass. Desperately hungry, with the two women seriously ill and Buck dying, they stopped to buy food. Within minutes the police were upon them and Buck was shot in the hip, shoulders and back. The police had found him, after the shoot-out, with his wife crouched over him, sobbing. Buck died in hospital six days later and Blanche was given a 10-year prison sentence.

Bonnie and Clyde spent the following three months desperately running from the police, but their luck could not hold out. On 23 May 1934 their Ford V-8 sedan was ambushed by six police officers. Their car was pumped full with 87 bullets and they died immediately, their bodies bloody and broken. Clyde was 25 and Bonnie just 23.

Incredibly, the glamorous legend of the two ruthless lovers had already begun. Vast crowds flocked to their funeral in Dallas, snatching flowers from the coffins as souvenirs. Time has done nothing to erase their memory, and despite their callous, cruel deeds, they are remembered by many as folk heroes.

The Fall River Axe Murders

LIZZIE BORDEN

According to the immortal rhyme, Lizzie Borden took an axe and gave her mother forty whacks; when she saw what she had done she gave her father forty one. But according to American justice, the 32-year-old spinster was not responsible for the bloody slaughter of Andrew J. Borden and his wife Abby. She was acquitted after a ten-day trial, and the courtroom rang with applause at the verdict. Ever since, the world has wondered why.

The Borden household at 92 Second Street in the Massachusetts cotton spinning town of Fall River had never been a happy one. Andrew was a crusty, puritanical character whose one aim in life was making money, and holding on to it. He had amassed half a million dollars from shrewd business dealings, first as an undertaker, then as a property speculator and banker. His first wife, Sarah Morse Borden, died in 1862, two years after giving birth to his second daughter, christened Lizzie Andrew because Borden wanted a boy. Borden married again two years later, but it was no love match. Abby Durfee Gray was a plain, plump woman of 37, more of a housekeeper than a wife. And there was no love lost between her and Borden's two girls. The elder sister Emma called her Abby. Lizzie called her Mrs Borden, refused to eat at the same table as her, and spoke with her only when it was essential.

Despite Borden's wealth, the family lived in conditions worse than many of the town's humble millworkers. The unsanitary whitewood house had staircases at the front and back, which was as well, because the friction in the family meant that bedroom doors upstairs were kept locked at all times, the parents reaching their room via the rear stairs, the girls using the front ones.

Lizzie's resentment of her stepmother, and the way they lived, boiled over when her father, whom she loved dearly, put up the money for Abby's sister, Mrs Whitehead, to buy the house from which she faced eviction. Borden presented the title deeds to his wife, and when Lizzie found out, she regarded it as further proof that Mrs Borden was only after her father's riches. Shortly afterwards, Mr Borden arrived home from business to be told by Lizzie that his wife's bedroom had been ransacked by a burglar. He reported the incident to police, but soon cut short their inquiries when it became clear that Lizzie herself had done the damage during 'one of her funny turns'.

Lizzie was plain, introspective and repressed with genteel pretensions. The curly-haired redhead had a small circle of very close friends. Though she belonged to the Women's Christian Temperance Union, was treasurer and secretary of the local Christian Endeavour Society, and taught a Sunday School of Chinese men at the local Congregational church, she spent most of her time in more solitary pursuits – fishing, or merely brooding at her bedroom window. There was plenty for her to brood about.

In the summer of 1892 Fall River sweltered in a heatwave. In May the tedium of the Bordens' lifestyle was interrupted when intruders twice broke into outhouses at the bottom of their garden. Mr Borden's reaction was somewhat bizzare. Sure that the intruders were after Lizzie's pet pigeons, he took an axe to the birds and decapitated them.

By August the heat had become so bad that Emma left to stay with friends in the country at Fairhaven, 20 miles away. Lizzie stayed at home for a special meeting of the Christian Endeavour Society. The weather made no difference to Mr Borden's plans for running an economical household. The family sat down to a monstrous joint of mutton, cooked by their only servant, an Irish girl called Bridget, and served up in various guises at every meal. Everyone except Lizzie was violently ill.

Although 4 August dawned as the hottest day of the year, the family routine went on just the same. After breakfast Mr Borden set out to check on his businesses; John Morse, brother of his first wife, who was staying for a few days, left to visit other relatives; Mrs Borden began dusting the rooms, and Bridget, still queasy from food poisoning, washed the windows. Lizzie came down later than the rest, and was soon seen ironing some clothes in the kitchen.

Shortly after 09.30, Mrs Borden, on her knees dusting in the spare bedroom upstairs at the front of the house, was struck from behind with a hatchet. It was a

---

Mystery will always surround 44-year-old Gilles de Rais, branded one of history's most shocking sadists. Once a lieutenant of Joan of Arc and a Marshal of France, he turned a life of near obscurity to one of notoriety.

He derived pleasure from sexual attacks on children and occasionally heightened the excitement by torturing or decapitating them first.

More than 120 children came into his evil clutches – all were first kidnapped then brutally murdered. After each of his sadistic adventures he sank into a coma. Finally, in 1440 he was sentenced to be strangled and then burned.

The axe allegedly used by Lizzie Borden

crushing blow to the head, and killed her instantly. But 18 more blows were inflicted on her before she was left in a room awash with blood.

Just before 11.00, Mr Borden arrived home to find the front door locked and bolted. Bridget the maid, by now cleaning the windows inside the house, went to let him in, and expressed surprise that the door was double locked. She heard a laugh behind her, and turned to see Lizzie coming down the front staircase, smiling.

Mr Borden was nearly 70, and walking in the morning heat had clearly tired him. Lizzie fussed round him, told him his wife had gone out after receiving a note about a sick friend, and settled him on the living room settee where he began to doze, his head resting on a cushion. Lizzie went back to the kitchen, and chatted to Bridget about some cheap dress material on sale in town. But Bridget was still feeling unwell, and decided to retire to her attic bedroom for a while. She heard the clock strike 11.00 as she went up the back stairs.

Ten minutes later she dashed downstairs again. She heard Lizzie shouting: 'Come down quick. Father's dead. Someone came in and killed him.' Lizzie would not let the maid into the living room – she sent her across the road to fetch the local doctor, a man called Bowen. He was out on a call. Lizzie then sent Bridget to fetch Alice Russell, one of her closest friends. By this time, the maid's rushing about had attracted the attention of neighbours. Mrs Adelaide

Churchill, who lived next door, spotted Lizzie looking distressed, and asked what was wrong. She was told: 'Someone has killed father.'

Mr Borden had been hacked to death in exactly the same way as his wife, though his head had been shattered with only ten blows. The hatchet had landed from behind as he slept, a tricky task as the settee was against a wall. Blood had splashed everything – wall, settee, floral carpet. Dr Bowen arrived and examined the body. The blows seemed directed at the eyes, ears and nose. He was completely satisfied the first blow had killed the old man. He placed a sheet over the body.

Mrs Russell and Mrs Churchill did their best to comfort the bereaved Lizzie, fanning her, dabbing her face with cold cloths, rubbing her hands. But both noticed that she did not really need comforting. She was not crying or hysterical, and she assured them she did not feel faint. She was still strangely calm when the police arrived, declining their offer of delaying the necessary interview until she had had a chance to rest.

At first suspicion fell on John Morse, who behaved strangely when he returned to the house. Though a large and excited crowd had gathered in front of the building, he was seen to slow down as he approached. Then, instead of going inside, he wandered round to the back garden, picked some fruit off one of the trees, and started munching it. Inside the house, his alibi came so glibly, in the most minute detail, that it almost seemed too perfect. But when tested it was found to be true.

Attention then turned to Lizzie, whose behaviour had been equally strange, and whose statements were not only curious but contradictory. When Bridget had asked her where she was when her father was killed, she replied: 'I was out in the yard and heard a groan.' When Mrs Churchill asked the same question, she said: 'I went out to the barn to get a piece of iron.' She told the same story to the police, saying she had eaten three pears while searching in the attic of the barn. But a policeman who checked the attic found no cores, only undisturbed dust.

Mrs Churchill also recalled the extraordinary reply Lizzie had given when she first arrived, and asked where her mother was. Lizzie said: 'I'm sure I don't know, for she had a note from someone to go and see somebody who is sick. But I don't know perhaps that she isn't killed also, for I thought I heard her coming in.' It was some minutes before Mrs Churchill and Bridget began to search for Mrs Borden. They knew she was not in her own room, for the sheet that covered her husband came from there. So they started climbing the front staircase. Halfway up, Mrs Churchill glanced through the open door of the spare bedroom, and saw the body lying on the floor beyond the bed.

Why had Lizzie not seen it there when she came down the stairs to welcome her father home? Why had she been trying to buy prussic acid, a lethal poison, only the day before from shops in town? And why, the previous evening, had she visited her friend Mrs Russell, told her of the food poisoning episode, and complained about her father's brusque way with people, saying she was afraid one of his enemies would take revenge on him soon?

Those were the questions police asked themselves as they pieced together the clues, and studied Lizzie's statements. They were sure that the murders had been committed by someone in the household. Though neighbours had noticed a young man outside the Borden home at 09.30, looking agitated, they had not seen him go in. And police thought it unlikely that a killer could hide in the house for 90 minutes between the murders while Bridget and Lizzie were going about their chores.

Bridget was considered as a suspect and dismissed. Neighbours had seen her cleaning the windows. Some had even seen her vomitting because of the food poisoning. And she had no known reason for killing her employers. But Lizzie had motives in plenty. The tension in the family, the quarrels about money, the hatred of the stepmother, were all well known in the area. She was warned that she was under suspicion and told not to leave the house. She accepted the conditions, in the arrogant, off-hand way that she had dealt with all the police's questions.

The police obtained a warrant for her arrest, but did not serve it until after the inquest. Though they had found an axe-head that had recently been cleaned in the cellar of the Borden house, they had no proof that it was the murder weapon, or that Lizzie was the murderer. Once she was arrested, she could use her legal right to silence. It was important to hear her evidence at the inquest.

More than 4,000 people attended the funeral of Mr and Mrs Borden. The two heads were cut off before burial, and the battered skulls sent for forensic examination. A few days later, the inquest opened. It was held in secret, conducted by the public prosecutor, who gave Lizzie a tough time in cross-questioning. And once again she started contradicting herself.

She claimed now that she had not been on the stairs when her father arrived home shortly before 11.00, but was downstairs in the kitchen. Asked why she had changed her story, she explained: 'I thought I was on the stairs, but now I know I was in the kitchen.' She also denied saying she heard her stepmother returning to the house. The public prosecutor was certain she was guilty of the killings. So were the newspapers, which daily poured out torrents of emotional calumny on Lizzie, adding smears and lies to the known facts. But it was one thing to obtain a conviction in print, quite another to win one in a court of law. And the public prosecutor confided in a letter to the Attorney General that he was not confident.

His fears were well founded. The tide of anti-Lizzie propaganda in the press turned public feeling in her favour. How could such a God-fearing, quiet,

Lizzie Borden

Brush manufacturer Henry Wainwright tired of his mistress, slit her throat and shot her. Then he buried her in his shop. When he became bankrupt a year later he dug up her body and to his horror found she was still 'intact'. He had buried her in chloride of lime instead of quicklime. Wainwright then meticulously chopped up the body and put the pieces into parcels to await disposal. But when he went in search of a London cab, a workman picked up one of the parcels and a hand fell out. Wainwright was executed at Newgate in 1875.

respectable girl do such horrible and bloody deeds? Flowers and good luck messages began pouring into Fall River for her from all over the country. Suddenly the state was the villain of the piece for persecuting her.

Lizzie had something else on her side also. She hired the best lawyer in Massachusetts, George Robinson, a former governor of the state. One of the three trial judges was a man Robinson had elevated to the bench while governor. He owed the defence lawyer a favour – and he delivered. The judges refused to allow evidence of Lizzie's attempts to buy prussic acid, saying it was irrelevant to the case, and they ruled that transcripts of her questioning at the inquest were inadmissable.

Lizzie's friends also rallied round. Both Emma and Bridget gave favourable evidence, playing down Lizzie's enmity for her stepmother. Mrs Russell admitted that Lizzie had burnt one of her dresses the day after her parents' funeral, but insisted there were no blood stains on it. Lizzie, too, played her part perfectly in court. When she fainted halfway through the hearing, there was an outcry at the way she was being tortured. And as she stood in the dock, modest, refined, neatly dressed, it was easy for George Robinson to say to the jury: 'To find her guilty, you must believe she is a fiend. Gentlemen, does she look it?'

The jury agreed she did not. After a ten-day trial her ordeal was over, and she was whisked off for a lavish celebration party, laughing at newspaper clippings of the hearing that friends gave her. She was now very rich, able to inherit her murdered father's wealth, but surprisingly she chose to stay on in Fall River, buying a larger house in the better part of town. Bridget, whom many suspected of helping Lizzie to dispose of clues to the killings, returned to Ireland, allegedly with a lot of money from the Borden bank account. She later returned to America and died in Montana in 1947, aged 82.

For a while Emma shared the new home with Lizzie, but the sisters quarrelled, and Emma moved out. Lizzie became something of a recluse, living alone, unloved and whispered about, until she died in 1927, aged 67. Emma, nine years older, died a few days later. They were both buried in the family plot, alongside their real mother, their stepmother, their father and their sister Alice, who had died as a child.

Can Lizzie rest in peace beside the victims of that hot morning in August, 1892? No-one else was ever arrested for the murders. No-one else was even seriously suspected. The case has become one of the most intriguing unresolved mysteries in the annals of crime. Five stage plays, a ballet, and countless books have been written about it. Opinions range from those who say she was a cunning, calculating killer who twice stripped naked to ensure her butchery left no blood-stained clothes, to the Society of Friends of Lizzie Borden, which still exists today to persuade us she was innocent.

Perhaps, in a way, she was. In her book *A Private Disgrace*, American authoress Victoria Lincoln argues convincingly that Lizzie committed the murders while having attacks of temporal epilepsy, the 'funny turns' her family were accustomed to. Lizzie suffered attacks four times a year, usually during menstruation. Miss Lincoln says: 'During a seizure, there are periods of automatic action which the patient in some cases forgets completely and in other remembers only dimly.' That could explain Lizzie's confusing statements and her coolness when accused of the killings.

Miss Lincoln even suggests the trigger to Lizzie's attacks. A note was delivered to 92 Second Street on the morning of 4 August, but it was not from a sick friend. It was to do with the transfer of a property to Mrs Borden's name. The first such transaction had driven Lizzie to vandalism. Did the second drive her to murder?

The Moors Murders

IAN BRADY AND MYRA HINDLEY

I t was the Swinging Sixties and everyone was into wild fashion, weird cults and *The Beatles*. But it wasn't long before Britain was stunned by what were labelled the most cold-blooded killings of the century. Even 20 years later, the horror was still etched in peoples' minds. A country could not forget Myra Hindley and Ian Brady, perpetrators of the notorious Moors Murders.

The 27-year-old stock clerk and 22-year-old typist committed some of the most macabre crimes ever recounted before a British jury. Britain of the sixties was hypnotised by the couple's blood-lust, of how they enticed young children back to their home, sadistically tortured them, murdered them and then buried their bodies on the desolate Pennine moors.

The couple's terrible crimes were committed while capital punishment was still in force but they were found guilty after its abolition. A short year separated them from the gallows and sentenced them to a life behind bars.

Many years later, reformers, such as Lord Longford, were to argue for Hindley's release. The brassy blonde, once infatuated by her lover was said to have undergone a startling change. In her 20 years in Holloway Prison she had turned to religion and taken and passed an Open University degree in humanities. She had, said Longford and his supporters, reached the point where she was no longer a danger to the public.

In 1973, Hindley was given her first taste of freedom since her life sentence – 'life' in Britain normally being 10 years with the possibility of release on licence at the Home Secretary's approval after a third had been served. Along with a prison officer, she was taken on early morning excursions to a London park, but her bouts of freedom raised a howl of protest from the public who could neither forgive or forget the killing of the innocents.

It was Myra Hindley's brother-in-law, David Smith, who eventually gave away the perverted couple's secrets. On 7 October, 1965 at 6.20 am, he contacted the police. The realization of what was going on at number 16, Wardle Brook Avenue on the Hattersley council estate, Manchester, was too strong for him to bear. Shaking, he walked to a public telephone kiosk and rang nearby Stalybridge police station. Within minutes, a young patrol car officer found Smith quaking beside the telephone box. He was so agitated that he could hardly wait to bundle himself into the officer's car.

Ian Brady

THE WORLD'S MOST INFAMOUS MURDERS

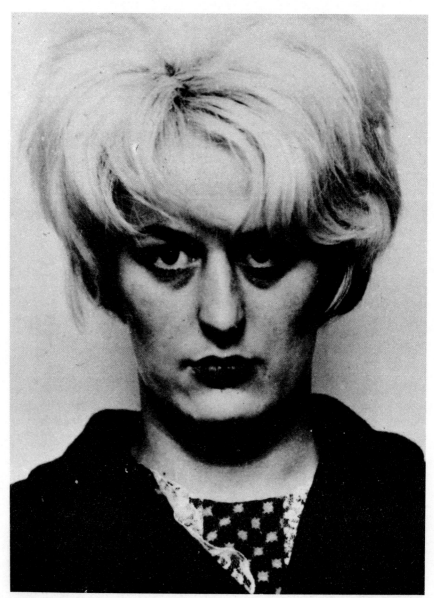

Myra Hindley

Alfred Stratton, 22, and his brother Albert, 20, were the first British murderers to be convicted by their fingerprints. It happened in May 1905, after the battered bodies of Thomas Farrow and his wife were found in the flat above their paint shop in south-east London. A right thumbprint was discovered on the forced cashbox, and after extensive inquiries the police found that it belonged to Alfred who, with his brother, was known to be a burglar.

At the Old Bailey trial, the defence argued strongly that fingerprints were inadmissible evidence, but the judge ruled otherwise. The two brothers were hanged.

As David Smith blurted out his tales of horror, one of the biggest searches ever seen in Britain was begun. Hundreds of police spent weeks scouring the desolate moors for the graves of 10-year-old Lesley Ann Downey and 12-year-old John Kilbride. John had vanished on 23 November, 1963 and Lesley had disappeared a year later, on Boxing Day, 1964.

But first the police had to gain entry to the house in Wardle Brook Avenue where the children had met their deaths. A police superintendent borrowed a white coat and basket from a bread roundsman and approached the house, which belonged to Hindley's grandmother. He knocked on the door which was opened by Hindley.

Brady was lying on a divan bed writing a letter. The note was to his employers saying he wouldn't be at work that day because he had injured his leg. At his trial, it was revealed he had planned to spend the day back on the moors – digging another grave.

With Brady and Hindley separated and safely behind bars, police concentrated all efforts on the moorland search. There they found the grave of 12-year-old John Kilbride. A few yards away, on the other side of a road which split the wild moorland in two, they found the remains of tiny Lesley Ann Downey. They were helped in their search by 'souvenir' photographs, taken by the couple, of Hindley standing over the two graves.

Then came the trial at Chester Assizes – and a courtroom and country shaken by tales of horror and torture. Brady and Hindley, it was revealed, kept vile photographs of their mutilated victims.

But nothing shocked the courtroom more than the playing of a tape. On it were the pleadings, the screams and last dying moments of Lesley Ann Downey.

It took the jury – all male – 18 days to listen to the most horrific evidence ever put before a British court. All seemed to lower their heads when prosecutor Sir Elwyn Jones, the Attorney General, played the tape of young Lesley Ann

THE WORLD'S MOST INFAMOUS MURDERS

> Cicero's tongue finally got the better of him in AD 43. The Roman orator was assassinated after vexing Mark Anthony with his caustic speeches. As a result, he lost his head and hands, which were displayed in Rome.
>
> Anthony's wife, Fulvia, took great glee in ripping Cicero's tongue out of his head and repeatedly stabbed it with a hairpin. She could never match his wit in life – but in death he could not answer back.

Downey's last moments. People in the court swayed with disgust and onlookers buried faces in their hands.

Brady, quizzed in the witness box, could only say that he was 'embarrassed' when he heard the tape. Hindley did not have her partner in crime's arrogance, but she still held her poise and confidence in the witness box. As her part in the killings became clear she kept uttering 'I was cruel. I was cruel'.

At precisely 2.40 pm on Friday, 6 May, the jury retired. For two hours and 20 minutes, they considered the verdict in 'the trial of the century'. Brady was given concurrent life-sentences for 'these calculated, cruel, cold-blooded murders'. Then came the final words that put Brady behind bars: 'Put him down'. Myra Hindley, for the first time, stood alone in the dock as the judge turned to her. She swayed, as if to faint as she too, was given life-sentences.

The Voyage of Terror

THOMAS BRAM

O n the stormy night of 13 July, 1896, Lester Monks, a passenger on the sailing ship *Herbert Fuller*, unlocked his door and stepped warily into the captain's cabin with a loaded revolver in his hand. He had been roused from sleep by what sounded like the scream of wind through the halyards. But wider awake, he knew it was more than that – a woman had been screaming.

The captain's cot had been toppled to its side and the skipper, Captain Charles Nash, lay dying in a pool of blood. His wife, Laura was on her bunk. Like Nash she had literally been chopped to death, her skull smashed in front and back and both jaws broken.

Monks staggered up the forward companionway to find the first mate, Thomas Bram, pacing the deck. And from the moment that he heard the news, Bram's conduct was bizarre. He refused to alert the second mate, August Blomberg, because he thought the man was inciting the crew against him. And in the end, incredibly, he slumped to the deck and hugged the passenger's legs, begging for protection.

At dawn they roused steward Jonathon Spencer and the three went to Blomberg's cabin. There they found the door wide open and the second mate hacked to death in his bunk, two of his severed fingers on the floor.

Surprisingly, Bram, who had by now assumed command of the ship, was able to lead them to the murder weapon on deck – a new axe sticky with blood and flesh. Still more strangely, the big man gave a throaty shriek and hurled the weapon overboard.

At a meeting of crew and passengers, Bram urged that the three bodies be thrown into the sea – an idea vetoed by all. He tried to blame the killings on the

---

Billy the Kid, whose real name may have been William Bonney or Henry McCarty, was reputed to have carried out 21 murders. It is now believed, however, that he killed 'only' four people. New York-born Billy was shot dead by Sheriff Pat Garrett, of Lincoln City, New Mexico, in 1881.

dead Blomberg, insisting that the second mate must have died of his own wounds. And he wanted to take the murder ship to French Guiana in South America.

An air of terror filled the big square-rigger, which had left Boston on 3 July bound for Argentina with a cargo of timber. In the six days that it took to return to port, no one aboard slept easily in his berth.

Bram managed to convince the crew that one of their members, Charley Brown, was acting suspiciously. If anything, the silent Brown looked relieved when they manacled him in a cabin. There were reasons why. Just before the ship reached Halifax, Brown told other crewmen he had seen the captain slain. As he had stood at the helm on that bloody night, the scene in the chartroom had been visible to him through a small window in front of the wheel. And afterwards, Brown said, he had heard Laura Nash screaming.

But he had kept the knowledge to himself because he was afraid of the maniac with the axe – their commander, First Mate Bram.

Bram's trial began in Boston on 14 December, 1896. Former shipmates testified that he had often approached them with the idea of killing various ship's officers and selling the stolen cargo. Bram himself boasted of looting two other vessels.

Sentenced to the gallows, he won a new trial on technical grounds and was committed to the U.S. penitentiary in Atlanta. He would have stayed there except for one thing – the strange intervention of mystery writer Mary Roberts Rinehart, author of *The Bat*, *The Cat and The Canary*, and other thrillers.

Mrs Rinehart had managed to convince herself that Bram was an abused innocent who had been framed by his shipmates. She wove the notion into a sensational novel, *The After House*, and managed to convince President Woodrow Wilson that she was right.

Thomas Bram was pardoned in 1919.

Convicted by his Crooked Teeth

THEODORE BUNDY

Law student Theodore Bundy was tall, handsome, charming and well educated, but this gentle, polite young man, with the looks to make girls swoon and the old-fashioned courtesy to appeal to their parents, was consigned to Death Row. The all-American boy Bundy is believed to be one of the worst mass murderers in American history – responsible for the savage rape and killing of 36 young women. Authorities in four states are convinced that beneath his disarming appearance lurked a Jekyll and Hyde. His victims were raped, clubbed, strangled and beaten to death. Investigators found that in every case Bundy had been nearby.

Bundy collected three death sentences in different trials. He was sentenced for the murders of two students in a Tallahassee sorority house in 1978, for the kidnap and murder of a Salt Lake City police chief's 12-year-old daughter, and for the kidnapping and battering of an 18-year-old girl out shopping in Salt Lake City. Yet the college graduate, who has planned to become a lawyer, always maintained his innocence. 'I have never killed, never kidnapped, never desired to injure another human being', he told a court.

The bloody trail of murders which bogged Bundy's footsteps began in 1974, when six strikingly similar and attractive young women vanished in the Seattle area. In January the first girl vanished from her bedroom. The only hint of her fate was a bloodstain on her pillow. Then in March a 19-year-old chemistry student left her dormitory at Evergreen State College for a concert. She was never seen again. A month later the third girl left her college to go to the cinema. She too never returned. In May and June three more girls vanished. No traces have ever been found of them.

All the girls were shapely brunettes. The other common factor was that each had been approached on the beach during the summer by a young, handsome man. He called himself Ted. There were no other clues to the disappearances until some forestry students strolling in the countryside found a jawbone and other bones in a shallow grave.

The discovery of the bones sent shock waves through the community. Detectives made little progress. But they later linked the murders with the disappearance of two more girls. The girls went missing at a picnic park. Three months later their corpses were found 10 miles from the other grave. Again

THE WORLD'S MOST INFAMOUS MURDERS

Drunken gunslinger Jack Slade was notorious for his savage
killing of Jules Bene, an old enemy who had once ambushed and
shot him. Slade took a slow revenge when they met again. He
fastened Bene to a post and, between swigs of whisky, shot at his
limbs. Then he blasted off his head and cut off an ear as a key fob.
   But it was not the murder of Jules Bene that finished Slade. It
was his drunken gun-slinging antics around Virginia City,
Montana, whose townsfolk hanged him from the main beam of
the saloon in 1864.
   His wife soaked the corpse in raw alcohol for the long trip to his
native Illinois. But he never made it. Slade's decomposed body
ended up in a Mormon cemetary in Salt Lake City.

witnesses talked of the mysterious and charming young man called Ted who
had been seen before the girls vanished.

Theodore Bundy was never charged with these murders. But he was arrested
for the attempted abduction of a 17-year-old girl. He was left alone in a
courtroom during a recess and he escaped. He was recaptured but he escaped
again. By this time Bundy was awaiting trial for the murders of a Michigan
nurse and a policeman's 14-year-old daughter. His escape launched a
nationwide hunt by police, who already suspected him of being a mass
murderer. But no trace was found of him until seven months later when four
students in a sorority house on Florida State University campus were
bludgeoned with a broken tree branch. Two of the girls died. After a hunt,
Bundy was arrested.

The trial which followed was one of the most sensational in American history.
The entire nation followed the proceedings on television, which under Florida
law was allowed into the courtroom. The bizarre twists in the case attracted
newsmen from around the world.

Bundy was convicted after evidence about the one flaw in his perfect
appearance. He had distinctly crooked teeth. And it was those teeth that gave
him away.

Evidence from a dental expert proved that bite marks on the body of one of
Bundy's victims matched his teeth. As one of the girls lay dying she had been
brutally bitten on her breast and buttock. The other dead girl had been
battered and strangled – so violently that a police witness said at first he thought
she had been decapitated.

When the verdict was announced, Bundy's mother shrieked in anguish and
screamed out that he was innocent. But Bundy, who was baptized as a Mormon
just before the murder spree began, was described as the 'most vicious criminal

CONVICTED BY HIS CROOKED TEETH

in history' by a Utah police captain who investigated some of the murders.

The personality of Bundy remains a mystery. To those who watched him calmly facing the death penalty in courtrooms, it seemed incredible that he could be the same man who battered women to death in frenzied sprees of violence. He was born in a home for unmarried mothers. But after that his background was impecable. He was a Boy Scout and worked as an assistant programmes director at the Seattle Crime Commission, where he battled against white-collar crime. He even helped write a booklet for women on rape prevention.

One person still convinced of his innocence is Carole Boone who married Bundy in a hurried ceremony in a court in Florida just before he was handed his third death sentence. Carole, who has kissed her husband only once, would drive regularly the 150 miles from her home to Talahassee where Bundy waited in a Death Row cell. She knew him before he was arrested and said: 'Ted is not vicious or a savage mass murderer. The charges were the result of snowballing hysteria on the part of law enforcement people looking for a fall guy on whom they could pin all their unsolved crimes. From the beginning, I believed in his innocence. When I looked into the evidence, I was convinced of it'. But the jurors who decided Bundy should die for the murders he committed feared that if he remained alive he might break out of jail and 'do it all a second time'.

The 'Monster in Human Shape'

MARY ANN COTTON

Welfare worker Thomas Riley walked briskly through the early morning summer sunshine. It was 06.00 and he was on his way to another day's duties at the village workhouse in West Auckland. Times were hard for the people of County Durham, and Riley was kept busy trying to care for those who could not cope. As he turned into Front Street, he recalled the widow at No 13. She had come to him only six days earlier, asking if he had room in the workhouse for her seven-year-old stepson, Charles Edward. 'It is hard to keep him when he is not my own, and he is stopping me from taking in a respectable lodger,' she said. Riley joked about the identity of the lodger. Was it the excise officer village gossips said she wanted to marry? 'It may be so,' the woman had replied, 'but the boy is in the way.'

Now, as he walked to work, Riley noticed the widow in the doorway of her three-room stone cottage. She was clearly upset, and he crossed the road to ask why. He could not believe his ears at what she told him: 'My boy is dead.'

Riley went straight to the police and the local doctor. What he told them was the first step in an investigation that was to brand the widow, Mary Ann Cotton, the worst mass murderer Britain had ever seen.

Riley was suspicious about the death because the lad had seemed in perfect health when he saw him six days earlier. Dr Kilburn was also surprised to hear of the tragedy. He and his assistant Dr Chambers had seen the boy five times that week for what they thought were symptoms of gastro-enteritis, but they never thought the illness could be fatal. Dr Kilburn decided to withhold a death certificate and asked for permission to carry out a post-mortem examination. The coroner agreed to the request, and arranged an inquest for the following afternoon, Saturday, 13 July, 1872.

The pressures of their practice meant the two doctors could not start their post-mortem until an hour before the hearing. After a cursory examination, Dr Kilburn told the jury in the Rose and Crown Inn, next to Cotton's house: 'I have found nothing to suggest poisoning. Death could have been from natural causes, possibly gastro-enteritis.' The jury returned a verdict of natural death, and Charles Edward was buried in a pauper's grave.

But Dr Kilburn had taken the precaution of preserving the contents of the boy's stomach in a bottle. On the following Wednesday he at last had time to put them to proper chemical tests. He went straight back to the police with the results. There were distinct traces of arsenic. Next morning, widow Cotton was arrested and charged with murder. The boy's body was dug up and sent to Leeds School of Medicine, where Dr Thomas Scattergood, lecturer in forensic medicine and toxicology, discovered more arsenic, in the bowels, liver, lungs, heart and kidneys.

Meanwhile, Thomas Riley was pointing out to the authorities that the death of Charles Edward was not the first in the family. In fact, there had been four in the two years since Mary Ann Cotton, a former nurse, had arrived in West Auckland. Her fourth husband, coal miner Frederick Cotton, died from 'gastric fever' on 19 September, 1871, two days after their first wedding anniversary. He was 39. Then, between 10 March and 1 April, 1872 10-year-old Frederick, Cotton's son by a previous marriage, Robert, Mary Ann's 14-month-old son, and Mary Ann's former lover, Joseph Nattrass, who had moved in with her again, all died. Gastric fever was again the cause of death on their certificates, except for the baby, who died from 'teething convulsions.'

Those three bodies were exhumed while Mary Ann waited for her trial in Durham Jail, and Dr Scattergood found traces of arsenic in all of them. Newspapers began looking more closely at the life of the miner's daughter from the Durham pit village of Low Moorsley. They unearthed a horrifying dossier of an apparently kind, good-natured and devout Methodist who seemed to spread death wherever she went.

In 1852, aged 20, she had married a labourer called William Mowbray, and moved to Devon. She had five children there, but four died. The couple returned to the north-east, moving from house to house in the Sunderland area, while Mary Ann worked at the town's infirmary. They had three more children. All died. Then Mowbray died. Mary Ann married again. Her husband, an engineer called George Wood, died in October 1866, 14 months after the wedding.

A month later, Mary Ann moved in as housekeeper to widower James Robinson and his three children. She soon became pregnant and married Robinson. But within weeks of her arrival in the household, Robinson's 10-month-old son John was dead. On 21 April, 1867, Robinson's son James, six, went to his grave. Five days later, his sister Elizabeth, eight, followed him. And on 2 May, nine-year-old Isabella, the only survivor of Mary Ann's marriage to Mowbray, lost her life.

Mary Ann had two daughters by Robinson. The first died within days of birth. The second was given away to a friend when the marriage broke up. Robinson survived, possibly because he resisted his wife's pleas to take out insurance on his life. But others who knew Mary Ann were not so lucky. She went to visit her mother because she feared she 'might be about to die'. No-one

> **Morbid American cannibal Albert Fish enjoyed a variety of dishes. The quiet painter and decorator confessed to having slaughtered six children – although the true total may have been 15. Most of the tender little bodies he swooped on were carefully cut up and stewed with vegetables. In the electric chair at Sing Sing in 1936, Fish seemed quite excited about being roasted himself – and even helped the executioner fix the electrodes.**

else was worried about the apparently sprightly 54-year-old, but within nine days she was dead. Mary Ann moved on, laden with clothes and bed linen.

She met and became friends with Margaret Cotton, and was introduced to her brother Frederick. Mary Ann quickly became pregnant, and married her new lover bigamously – her third husband, Robinson, was still alive. The wedding was slightly marred by the unexpected death of Margaret, whose £60 bank account went to the newly-weds. In all, 21 people close to Mary Ann lost their lives in less than 20 years. She had given birth to 11 children, yet only one survived – the girl she gave away. Small wonder, then, that on the morning of her trial, a local newspaper, unfettered by today's laws of libel and contempt, ran the headline: 'The Great Poisoning Case At West Auckland – Horrible Revelations'. But when she stepped into the courtroom at Durham Assizes shortly before 10.00 on 5 March, 1873, she was charged only with one killing, that of her stepson, Charles Edward.

The prosecution, led by Sir Charles Russell, later to become Lord Chief Justice, alleged the 40-year-old widow had poisoned the boy because there was a Prudential Insurance policy on his life worth £8, and because he was an impediment to her marraige to her excise officer lover, a man called Quick-Manning, by whom she was already pregnant. 'She was badly off and Charles Edward was a tie and burden to her,' said Sir Charles.

Mary Ann Dodds, a former neighbour of the accused, told the court she had bought a mixture of arsenic and soft soap from one of the village's chemist's shops in May 1872, two months before the boy's death. 'The mixture was needed to remove bugs from a bed in Mary Ann's home,' she said. 'I rubbed most of it into the joints of the bed and the iron crosspieces underneath.'

Chemist John Townend said the mixture would have contained about an ounce of arsenic – about 480 grains. Three grains were enough to kill an adult. He also thought it significant that his shop was not the closest chemist's to widow Cotton's home.

Thomas Riley gave his evidence about Mary Ann's eagerness to get the boy off her hands, and Dr Kilburn explained the medical steps he had taken. It was then that controversy entered the trial. The prosecution wanted to introduce evidence of earlier deaths in the family. Defence lawyer Thomas Campbell Foster, appointed only two days before the trial because Cotton could not afford her own legal representation, protested that his client was charged with only one death, which he maintained was an accident caused by arsenic impregnation of some green floral wallpaper. To discuss the earlier deaths would prejudice a fair trial, he said.

But Judge Sir Thomas Archibald ruled against him, citing legal precedent. From that moment on, the verdict was a foregone conclusion. The defence introduced no witnesses, and at 18.50 on the third day of the trial, the jury returned after only an hour's deliberations to pronounce Mary Ann Cotton guilty of murder.

The judge donned his black cap to sentence her to death, saying: 'You seem to have given way to that most awful of all delusions, which sometimes takes possession of persons wanting in proper moral and religious sense, that you could carry out your wicked designs without detection. But while murder by poison is the most detestable of all crimes, and one at which human nature shudders, it is one the nature of which, in the order of God's providence, always leaves behind it complete and incontestable traces of guilt. Poisoning, as it were, in the very act of crime writes an indelible record of guilt.'

They were fine words, but not strictly true. The state of medical knowledge in the 1870s was not as sophisticated as it is today. In an unsanitary age, gastric fever was a common killer, and overworked doctors could not examine every corpse without strong reasons. Though the final toll of deaths in Mary Ann's circle was high, she avoided suspicion by moving house frequently, and always calling in local doctors when her victims began complaining of stomach pains. The fact that she had once been a nurse, and was well known for caring for sick neighbours, also made people trust her.

No-one will ever know how many of the 21 unlucky people around her were poisoned either for insurance money, possessions, or because they stood in the way of a new marriage. Most people put the number of murders at 14 or 15. But despite the horror at what the *Newcastle Journal* newspaper described as 'a monster in human shape', many people had misgivings about her death sentence. There were doubts about hanging a woman, doubts about the way

---

Fugitive Leonard T. Fristoe was on the run from the law for 46 years. Jailed for life in 1920 for killing two deputy sheriffs, he served only three years of his sentence before escaping. His luck ran out when, at the ripe old age of 77, he was recaptured at Compton, California, after being turned in by his own son.

her defence in court had been organized, doubts about whether evidence of earlier deaths should have been allowed, doubts about the lack of any witnesses for the defence.

The *Newcastle Journal* admitted:

> 'Perhaps the most astounding thought of all is that a woman could act thus without becoming horrible and repulsive. Mary Ann Cotton, on the contrary, seems to have possessed the faculty of getting a new husband whenever she wanted one. To her other children and her lodger, even when she was deliberately poisoning them, she is said to have maintained a rather kindly manner.' The paper felt instinctively that the earth should be rid of her, but added: 'Pity cannot be withheld, though it must be mingled with horror.'

Mary Ann spent her last few days in jail trying to win support for a petition for a reprieve. She gave birth to Quick-Manning's daughter, Margaret, and arranged for her to go to a married couple who could not have children. Five days before her execution, the baby was forcibly taken from her. On 24 March, 1873, still maintaining her innocence, she went to the scaffold at Durham. It was three minutes before the convulsions of her body stopped.

Within eight days, a stage play, *The Life and Death of Mary Ann Cotton*, was being performed in theatres, labelled 'a great moral drama'. Mothers threatened recalcitrant children with the prospect of a visit from the West Auckland widow, and youngsters made up a skipping rhyme which began: 'Mary Ann Cotton, she's dead and rotten.' But she remains today one of the most enigmatic figures in the gallery of killers – a simple-minded mass murderer who evoked revulsion and sympathy in equal measures.

A Miscarriage of Justice?

JOHN CHRISTIE

John Reginald Halliday Christie was regarded by his neighbours as hard-working and respectable, although not particularly likeable. They often took his advice on medical matters, of which he affected a knowledge. It was also rumoured that he could help a girl terminate a pregnancy which may be why he apparently found it so easy to lure prostitutes to his home . . . and to their deaths.

For 14 years Christie lived in a run-down terraced house at 10 Rillington Place in London's decaying Notting Hill district. Christie and his wife Ethel had taken the ground-floor flat in 1938 at a time when he was trying to play down his five criminal convictions, one of which was for assaulting a woman. During the war he applied for a job as a reserve policeman and, because his record was never checked, he got it. After the war he worked briefly in a factory, then took a job as a post office clerk.

Christie's wife disappeared while the couple were living at number 10, and the solitary widower finally moved to another flat in 1952.

In March 1953 a prospective tenant was looking over the ground floor flat at 10 Rillington Place when he detected a foul smell which seemed to be emanating from a papered-over kitchen cupboard. Thinking that a rat had found its way inside and died, he ripped open the cupboard. What he found made him rush to the nearest telephone box and dial 999.

When the police arrived, they stripped the flat. In the kitchen cupboard they found the bodies of three prostitutes. Two more bodies were found buried in the back-yard. And beneath the sitting-room floor was the body of Ethel Christie.

Christie confessed to the six murders. In one of the most sensational and horrifying trials in history, it was said that he could gain sexual satisfaction only with dead women. Christie hoped to be found guilty but insane, and his life spared, but he was sentenced to death by hanging.

That, however, was far from being the end of the story. For as well as the six bodies found at 10 Rillington Place, Christie also confessed to murdering Beryl Evans, the wife of an ex-neighbour, Timothy Evans. The confession, however, came too late to help poor Timothy Evans, for in 1950 he had been sentenced to death by hanging – for murder.

To this day, no-one knows for sure which of the two men killed Beryl Evans.

A MISCARRIAGE OF JUSTICE?

Above left: 10 Rillington Place. Victims from left to right: Beryl Evans, Hectorina MacLennan, Muriel Amelia Eady, Kathleen Maloney, Rita Nelson, Ruth Fuerst Above right: John and Ethel Christie

THE WORLD'S MOST INFAMOUS MURDERS

Bible-loving Earle Leonard Nelson claimed he was 'a very religious man of high ideals'. But in less than two years, he raped and strangled at least 22 landladies across the United States and Canada in a trail of terror that began in San Francisco in February 1926, and ended in Winnipeg, Canada, in June 1927.
He was finally captured after changing his clothes at a secondhand store, and leaving behind a fountain pen taken from the home of his last victim, Mrs Emily Paterson. At his trial in Winnipeg, accused of her murder, he pleaded insanity. However, the jury decided that a man who kept on the move, changing his clothes and name after each killing, was not insane. He was hanged on 13 January, 1928, aged 36.

What is certain is that no jury today could possibly convict Timothy Evans of the crime.

Evan's confession was made on the spur of the moment when he walked into a police station in Merthyr Tydfil, South Wales, on 30 November, 1949, and told the officer at the desk: 'I would like to give myself up. I have disposed of the body of my wife.'

Evans, a gullible, illiterate van driver who ws largely under the spell of the evil Christie, told detectives that they would find his wife's body in a drain at 10 Rillington Place, where the Evans family had occupied the top-floor flat.

Police searched the house but could not find the dead woman in the drains. A later search, however, revealed the body in a small wash-house at the back of Number 10. She had been strangled, the same means of death meted out by Christie to all his victims. But more horrifying still was the discovery of a second corpse in the wash-house. It was the body of Evans's baby daughter, Geraldine. Evans appeared to be shattered by the discovery of his daughter. He at first admitted both murders but at his trial he accused Christie of the crimes.

The unfortunate Evans said that his wife was pregnant for the second time and that Christie had offered to give her an abortion. Evans agreed and left the two together. Afterwards, Christie showed Evans the woman's body and said that she had died during the abortion. He advised Evans to get rid of all his wife's clothes and other possessions and to leave London for a while. Meanwhile, Christie would arrange for little Geraldine to be unofficially adopted by a couple he knew. But apparently he decided to get rid of her, too.

That was Evans's story but the jury did not believe him. In court Christie, the ex-policeman, was a much more convincing witness. His previous conviction for viciously assaulting a woman was not mentioned to the jury. The prosecution described Christie as 'this perfectly innocent man'.

A MISCARRIAGE OF JUSTICE?

The simple-minded Evans was convicted – technically for murder of his baby only – and hanged. Christie stayed free for another three years . . . free to commit another four murders. He murdered his wife and then three prostitutes in close succession. Their bodies were added to those of the two women whom Christie had murdered in 1943 and 1944 and buried in the back-yard.

Christie was brought to justice in June 1953. He was tried for the murder of his wife and hanged at Pentonville Prison on 15 July, 1953.

But that was not the end of the story. Public outcry grew over the years for an inquiry into what was seen as a ghastly miscarriage of justice over the execution of Timothy Evans. But it was not until 1966 that pressure for an official review of the case succeeded in prompting the government to authorize an inquiry under Mr Justice Brabin. He ruled: 'It is more probable than not that Evans killed Beryl Evans, and it is more probable than not that Evans did not kill Geraldine.'

The ruling fell short of the sort of verdict that the pro-Evans campaigners had fought for over the years. But it did mean that Evans, whose conviction was for killing his daughter, could receive a posthumous royal pardon. His body was exhumed from Pentonville Prison and reburied in consecrated ground.

What the ruling did not do was to answer some extremely pertinent questions about the efficiency of the police, who failed to turn up the evidence that would, right from the start, have pointed the finger clearly at scheming, glib, persuasive mass-strangler Christie.

Why, when investigating Evan's allegations, did they fail to take note of Christie's previous record, happily accepting his wartime police service as evidence of his good character? Why did they unquestionably accept Christie's claim that he could not have helped dispose of Beryl Evans's body because his fibrositis prevented his lifting any heavy weight?

Why, on the first two occasions that police searched 10 Rillington Place for the body of Mrs Evans, did they not look in the wash-house? It was only on the third visit that they made their grisly discovery. And then only after standing with Christie in his back-yard and discussing with him the possibility of digging up his tiny garden to find out whether Beryl Evans was buried there.

If they had decided to dig up the yard, the detectives would have found the shallow grave of, not Mrs Evans, but the two other women who had been lured to the house, murdered and buried by Christie. As they chatted to Christie on that chill December morning in 1949, the detectives were standing on top of the two bodies. While the men spoke, Christie's small mongrel dog dug in the earth around their feet – and uncovered a woman's skull. Christie shooed the dog away and kicked earth over the evidence. The detectives noticed nothing.

If they had been more observant, four women might have been saved from murder, and Timothy Evans saved from the gallows.

The Strychnine Specialist

NEILL CREAM

Neill Cream had a surprise for the hangman when he mounted the scaffold on 15 November, 1892. He unexpectedly confessed that he was Jack the Ripper. But the authorities knew better. They realized it was just another attempt by the pathetic psychopath to glamourize his career as a killer. Cream described by one acquaintance as 'a degenerate with filthy desires and practices', certainly killed the same targets, in the same area, as the Ripper, but he did so in a style that was even more loathsome than that of London's most notorious murderer.

Cream was a pitiless sadist who revelled in drawing attention to his exploits. He committed the worst of his murders after being released from a life sentence in jail. Cream was born in Glasgow in 1850, but his parents emigrated to Canada when he was only four, and were prosperous enough to send him to Montreal's McGill College, where he qualified as a doctor in 1876.

But it was taking life, not saving it, that interested him most. He became an abortionist, a profitable though illegal trade in those days. Cream was doing well, until the father of Flora Brooks, a girl to whom he gave an abortion after making her pregnant, forced him at gun-point to marry her. The honeymoon lasted one day, before Cream left to continue his medical studies in London. The reluctant bridegroom returned after a year to find his wife dead of consumption. He again worked as an abortionist, adding blackmail as a sideline, but as his reputation grew more notorious, he moved south to the United States, to try his luck in Chicago. By 1880 he was known to the police. He was arrested for murder after Julia Faulkner, a girl whose pregnancy he aborted, died. He was, however, tried and cleared. Later two of his few legitimate patients died, the first a spinster who was going to Cream for medicine, the second an epileptic railway worker, Daniel Stott, whose wife collected pills for him, and enjoyed Cream's sexual favours, at the clinic.

The police were not suspicious about either death, until Cream went out of his way to attract their attention. He wrote to the coroner saying the chemist must have put too much strychnine in Stott's pills, and asking for the body to be exhumed. When it was, it soon became clear that the chemist was not responsible for doctoring the pills. Cream, who had eloped with Stott's widow, was arrested, and jailed for life for second degree murder.

Neill Cream

But in July 1891, after less than ten years, the governor of Illinois commuted the sentence, and Cream was released. His father had died, leaving him $16,000, and powerful friends of the family pulled strings to set him free to enjoy his new riches. Cream returned to Canada, but not for long. He soon sailed for England and the gas-lit streets of Lambeth where he had wandered as a student.

Cream had studied the career of Jack the Ripper, and was proud to walk where his hero had struck. He also had a penchant for prostitutes, boasting to acquaintances that he sometimes took on two at a time, or visited three in one night. But sex was not his only pleasure. He gave some girls pills which he said would cure the spots on their faces. In fact, they contained strychinine, the most agonizing of all poisons. And as the girls trustingly took them after he left, Cream got his kicks from imagining the excruciating pain of the victims as they writhed violenty before death.

Late in 1891, two young prostitutes, Elizabeth Masters and Elizabeth May, were watching for Cream from their window in Hercules Road, Lambeth. But as he walked towards their room, he was accosted by another lady of the night, Matilda Clover, aged 26, and followed her to her lodgings in Lambeth Road. Ten days later, on 20 October she died there in terrible pain, blurting that she had been poisoned by pills given to her by a man named Fred. But Matilda's doctor, who was treating her for alcoholism, wrote 'Natural Causes' on the death certificate.

Seven days earlier, on 13 October, Ellen Donworth, a 19-year-old prostitute, had been found in dreadful agony in Waterloo Road. Before she died on the way to hospital, she told of a tall man with cross-eyes and gold spectacles who had given her a bottle containing white fluid to drink. The man also wore a silk hat and had bushy whiskers. A post-mortem examination revealed that Ellen had been killed by strychnine.

Cream followed up his two murders with the curious correspondence that the British police only later realized was his trademark. He wrote in false names to Lord Russell and a Dr William Broadbent, accusing them both of killing Matilda. He demanded £2,500 from the doctor, under threat of exposing him. Broadbent went to the police, but the blackmailer never turned up as arranged. Cream also wrote to the coroner who was to hear the Ellen Donworth case, saying he had information about the murderer which he was prepared to sell for £300,000. Police consigned the letter, signed G. O'Brian, detective, to their idiot file.

What Cream's purpose was in writing the letters has never been discovered. Some experts in psychology say he wanted to keep his crimes in the public mind, inventing sensational sums of money merely to make the murders more newsworthy. Certainly he was never interested in collecting the sums he demanded. Others say he had a death wish, almost wanting to be arrested so he could bask in what he imagined to be the glory of public recognition. Perhaps also he remembered that Jack the Ripper had taunted his pursuers through the mail.

Cream sailed home to Canada in January 1892, after getting engaged to Laura Sabbatini, and whiled away the hours on board by bragging to fellow passengers about his sex life, the poisons he used to 'get women out of the family way' and the false whiskers he wore to make sure he was not recognized. Back in Canada, for no apparent reason, he had 500 posters printed. They read: 'Ellen Donworth's Death. To the guests of the Metropole Hotel: Ladies and Gentleman, I hereby notify you that the person who poisoned Ellen Donsworth on the 13th last October is today in the employ of the Metropole and that your lives are in danger as long as you remain in this hotel'. He signed the posters, 'Yours respectfully, W. H. Murray,' and datelined them 'London, April, 1892.' But why he picked on the Metropole Hotel was never explained. And, in fact, the posters were never distributed there.

Cream left New York for Liverpool on 23 March, and was back in Lambeth by 11 April, when he enjoyed a three-in-a-bed romp with 18-year-old Emma Shrivell and 21-year-old Alice Marsh. He left at 02.00, giving each girl three pills for her complexion. The two prostitutes died horribly that night, gasping to companions that the pills had come from a man called Fred.

The inquest verdict caused a sensation in a city still not certain that it had heard the last of Jack the Ripper. The two girls had been killed by strychnine. But again Cream could not leave well alone. And this time, it was to lead to the hangman's noose.

He wrote to a Dr Harper, accusing his son Walter, a medical student who lodged near Cream in Lambeth Palace Road, of causing the deaths of Alice and Emma. This time the price for suppressing the information was £1,500. Harper had nothing to fear, so he went to the police. They compared the handwriting with a letter Cream himself had given them. It was allegedly sent to Alice and Emma, warning them to beware of Dr Harper, who had killed Matilda and a certain Lou Harvey. The writing matched, and Cream was charged with attempted blackmail and false pretenses. Meanwhile, police exhumed Matilda Clover's body from her pauper's grave in Tooting. She too had died from strychnine, despite her doctor's diagnosis of natural causes.

Cream had made a fatal mistake – only Matilda's killer would have known that she had been murdered. By accusing another man, he had convicted himself. Elizabeth Masters and Elizabeth May were prepared to testify that they had seen Cream with her before her death. The police knew they had a cast iron case. Only one thing troubled them. Who was Lou Harvey? They arrested Cream on 3 June, charged him with murder, and set about finding out.

Lou Harvey, when discovered in Brighton, turned out to be the one girl who had cheated Cream's murderous plans. She had met him the previous October in London's Soho and spent the night with him at a hotel. Before he left next morning, he gave her some pills to clear up acne on her forehead, and arranged to meet her that evening near Charing Cross. Lou – short for Louisa – never took the pills. The man who lived on her earnings did not like the look of them, and forced her to throw them away. And when she kept the evening date, he was watching from a distance.

Cream bought the girl a drink and presented her with roses. He then gave her two more pills to take, but she managed to throw them away surreptitiously, and he seemed satisfied when he asked to see her hands, and they were empty. Cream left to enjoy his death agony fantasies – and seemed astonished, a month later, to see her alive and apparently well in Piccadilly.

Lou's story was added to the dossier against Cream, and on 17 October, 1892, the heartless poisoner went on trial at the Old Bailey. He had no credible evidence to offer against the accusations of Louisa and the two Elizabeths. A chemist testified that Cream had bought nux vomica, a vegetable product from which strychnine is extracted, and gelatin capsules. Police revealed that seven bottles of strychnine were found in Cream's lodgings. The jury took only 12 minutes to find him guilty. Nobody mourned when the rope put an end to his miserable life less than a month later.

Two curious claims kept Cream's name before the public for a while longer. In an extraordinary letter to *The Times*, his optician claimed that his moral degeneracy might have been avoided if his cross-eye defect had been corrected at an early age. And Sir Edward Marshall Hall, one of the most renowned advocates in British legal history, said he once successfully defended Cream against a charge of bigamy by claiming he was in prison in Sydney, Australia, at the time. The governor of the jail there confirmed that a man answering Cream's description had indeed been in his custody.

When Marshall Hall later learned that Cream had never been to Australia, he became convinced that the poisoner had a double in the underworld, and that the two look-alikes supplied alibis for each other when necessary. Some writers have even argued that the double may have been Jack the Ripper. But despite his claim on the scaffold, Cream could not have been the Ripper. For he had an unshakable alibi at the time of the Ripper's reign of terror in 1888 – he was serving a life sentence in Chicago's Joliet Prison.

Caught By A New Invention

DR CRIPPEN

No name in the annals of murder is more notorious than that of Dr Hawley Harvey Crippen. Yet Crippen killed only once and, but for three fatal errors, might have got away with it. He was a quiet, inoffensive little man, intelligent, courteous and kind with a touch of nobility about his actions. Perhaps that only served to enhance the horror of his ghastly crime.

Born in Coldwater, Michigan, in 1862, he studied long and hard for his medical degrees in Cleveland, Ohio, London and New York. He practised in several big American cities, and was already a widower when, at 31, he became assistant to a doctor in Brooklyn, New York. Among the patients there was a 17-year-old girl who called herself Cora Turner. Attractive and lively, she was the mistress of a stove manufacturer by whom she was pregnant. She miscarried.

Despite her circumstances, Crippen fell in love with her, and began trying to win her affections. He found that her real name was Kunigunde Mackamotzki, that her father was a Russian Pole and her mother a German, and that the girl wanted to be an opera singer. Crippen paid for singing lessons, though he must have known her dreams were bigger than her talent. They married in 1893.

In 1900, Crippen, now consultant physician to Munyon's, a company selling mail-order medicines, was transferred to England as manager of the head office in London. Later that year Cora joined him, and decided to switch her singing aspirations to music hall performances. She changed her name to Belle Elmore, and Crippen too took a new name. He dropped Hawley Harvey and called himself Peter.

Cora cultivated a large circle of Bohemian friends, dressing gaudily, bleaching her hair, and acquiring false blonde curls. She was extrovert and popular, particularly with men, and for a time her insignificant husband, small, slight and with an over-sized sandy moustache, was happy to observe her gay social whirl through his gold-rimmed spectacles, occasionally buying her furs or jewellery which he loved to present in front of her friends. The finery contrasted with the squalor of their home – neither had much inclination for household chores, and both were content to live in a dingy back kitchen, surrounded by

49

dirty crockery, piles of clothes, and two cats that were never let out.

Any bliss that there had been in this marriage of apparent opposites vanished while Crippen was away on the company's business in Philadelphia. He returned after several months to be told by Cora that she had been seeing an American music hall singer called Bruce Miller, and that they were fond of each other.

In September, 1905, the Crippens moved to 39 Hilltop Crescent, off Camden Road, in north London. It was a leafy street of large Victorian houses, enjoying its heyday as a good address, and cost £52 50p (£52 10s) rent a year – a large slice out of Crippen's £3 a week salary. But the new home did nothing to heal the growing rift between husband and wife. Crippen was to recall: 'Although we apparently lived very happily together, there were very frequent occasions when she got into the most violent tempers and often threatened she would leave me, saying she had a man she would go to and she would end it all. She went in and out just as she liked and did as she liked. I was rather a lonely man and rather miserable.' Soon they were sleeping in separate rooms.

Cora threw herself into working for the Music Hall Ladies Guild, pretending to be a big star helping the less lucky members of her profession via the charity organization. She also took a succession of lovers, some of whom gave her gifts and money. Crippen found consolation too, in the form of Ethel Le Neve, a secretary at Munyon's offices in New Oxford Street. She could not have been less like Cora. Quiet, lady-like, she craved respectability, and the doctor had to use all his powers of persuasion before she at last agreed to accompany him to a discreet hotel room for the first time. Thoughts of her kept Crippen's spirits up as life at home became even worse. His wife began taking in 'paying guests', and when he returned from work, he was expected to clean their boots, bring in their coal, and help with cleaning.

By 1909, Crippen was also a paying partner in a dental clinic, and his expenses, with two women to support, were strained. That November, he lost his job as Munyon's manager, and was paid only a commission for sales. The following month, Cora gave their bank 12 months notice that she was withdrawing the £600 in their joint deposit account. She did not need her husband's consent for that. Cora had also learnt of Crippen's affair with Ethel, and told friends she would leave him if he did not give the girl up.

On 17 January, 1910, Crippen ordered five grains of hyoscine from a chemist's shop near his office. The drug, a powerful narcotic used as a depressant in cases of mental or physical suffering, was then virtually unknown in Britain, and the chemist had none in stock. He delivered it to the doctor two days later.

On 31 January, the Crippens entertained two retired music hall friends to dinner and whist. It was, according to one of the guests, Clara Martinetti, 'quite

Dr. Crippen's wife

a nice evening and Belle was very jolly.' Clara and her husband Paul left at 01.30. Then, according to Crippen's later statements, Cora exploded with fury, threatening to leave home next day because he, Crippen, had failed to accompany elderly Mr Martinetti to the upstairs lavatory.

Cora Crippen was never seen alive again. On 2 February her husband pawned some of her rings for £80 and had Ethel Le Neve deliver a letter to the Music Hall Ladies Guild, saying that Cora, by now treasurer, would miss their next few meetings. She had rushed to America because a relative was seriously ill. On 9 February Crippen pawned more of his wife's gems, receiving £115. And soon her friends noticed still more of her jewels and clothes – being worn by Ethel Le Neve. She even went to the Guild's benevolent ball with Crippen, and wore one of Cora's brooches.

Inquiring friends started to get increasingly bad news about Belle Elmore from her husband. First she was uncontactable, 'right up in the wilds of the mountains of California.' Then she was seriously ill with pneumonia. And on 24 March, Crippen sent Mrs Martinetti a telegram just before he and Ethel left for a five-day Easter trip to Dieppe. It read: 'Belle died yesterday at six o'clock.' Two days later, notice of the death appeared in *The Era* magazine. Her body, according to Crippen, had been cremated in America.

Meanwhile, Ethel Le Neve had moved into 39 Hilldrop Crescent as housekeeper, bringing a French maid with her. She told her own landlady that Crippen's wife had gone to America. Clearly she was not likely to come back – Ethel left half her wardrobe behind, expecting to use Cora's clothes.

Crippen had given his own landlord notice of quitting, but he grew more confident as the constant questions about Cora tailed off, and so extended his lease until September. Then, on 28 June, came the first of what would prove fatal blows. A couple called Nash arrived back from touring American theatres, and told Crippen they had heard nothing of Cora's death while in California. Unhappy with his answers, they spoke to a highly-placed friend of theirs in Scotland Yard.

In 1914 society beauty Henriette Caillaux, wife of the French finance minister, shot dead Gaston Calmette, editor of the newspaper *Le Figaro*. Henriette had become enraged over a campaign against her husband by Calmette, who in two months had written 130 vitriolic articles about the minister. The final straw came when *Le Figaro* printed a revealing love letter written to Henriette by Caillaux before their marriage. The trial jury obviously sympathized with her. Henriette, who claimed her gun had fired by mistake, was acquitted.

CAUGHT BY A NEW INVENTION

Brian Donald Hume, a 39-year-old racketeer and psychopath, knew that he could not be tried for murder twice. He had been arrested for chopping up his business partner, Stanley Setty, and throwing the bits from a plane over the English Channel. He was cleared of murder but admitted to being an accessory and collected a 12-year sentence.

In 1958 Hume sold his confession to a Sunday newspaper and went off to Switzerland where he began a new career as a bank robber. In Zurich he murdered a taxi driver and, while awaiting trial, penned a novel *The Dead Stay Dumb*. Sentenced to life imprisonment in 1976, Hume was sent back to Britain where he was declared insane and despatched to Broadmoor.

On Friday 8 July, Chief Inspector Walter Dew and a sergeant called at Crippen's office, and asked to know more about Cora. Did her husband have a death certificate? Crippen admitted that the story of her death was a lie, designed to protect her reputation. She had, in fact, run off to America to join another man, probably her old flame Bruce Miller. The doctor dictated a long statement over five hours, broken only for amicable lunch with the policemen at a nearby restaurant. He readily agreed to accompany the officers back to Hilldrop Crescent for a search of the house. Dew was mildly puzzled that Mrs Crippen had left behind all her finest dresses, but he left satisfied nothing was amiss.

Crippen did not know that, however. He panicked, and made what would prove to be his biggest mistake. Overnight, he persuaded Ethel to leave with him for a new life in America. Early next morning, he asked his dental assistant to clear up his business and domestic affairs, then sent him out to buy some boy's clothes. That afternoon Crippen and Ethel left for Europe.

On the following Monday, Chief Inspector Dew returned to ask Crippen to clarify a few minor points in the statement, and discovered what had happened. Alarmed, he instantly ordered a more thorough search of Crippen's house and garden. At the end of the second day, Dew himself discovered a loose stone in the floor of the coal-cellar. Under it he found rotting human flesh, skin and hair, but no bones.

A team of top pathologists from St Mary's hospital, Paddington, painstakingly examined the remains, and decided they were of a plump female who bleached her hair. Part of the skin came from the lower abdomen, and included an old surgical scar in a position where Mrs Crippen was known to have one. The remains also contained huge traces of hyoscine, which kills within 12 hours if taken in excess. On 16 July, warrants for the arrest of Crippen and Ethel were issued. They were wanted for murder and mutilation.

Crippen had made two errors. He had carved out the bones of the body, and presumably burned them in his kitchen stove. But he had treated the fleshy remains with wet quicklime, a corrosive substance only effective when dry. And he had wrapped them before burial in a pyjama jacket with the label 'Shirtmakers, Jones Brothers, Holloway.' All might still have been well but for his third error, fleeing.

The discovery of the body aroused horrified indignation in the British press, but the two runaways, staying in Rotterdam and Brussels, did not realize the storm had broken. On 20 July, they left Antwerp in the liner *SS Montrose*, bound for Quebec. Crippen had shaved off his moustache and discarded his glasses, and was posing as John Philo Robinson, while Ethel, dressed in the boy's clothes Crippen's assistant had bought, pretended to be his 16-year-old son, John. But if they thought they were safe, they were wrong.

The ship's commander, Captain Kendall, had read all about the gruesome findings at Hilldrop Crescent, and was aware that the *Daily Mail* had offered £100 for information about the couple the police were hunting. Kendall noticed an inordinate amount of hand-touching between Mr Robinson and his son. The boy's suit fitted badly, and he seemed almost lady-like when eating meals, when his father would crack nuts for him or offer him half his salad.

Kendall surreptiously collected up all the English-language papers on board so as not to alarm the couple. He checked Crippen's lack of reaction when he called him Robinson, and invited the couple to dine at his table. After two days at sea, he sent a message to the ship's owners over the newly-installed wireless telegraph, reporting his suspicions. On 23 July, Chief Inspector Dew and his sergeant set sail from Liverpool in the *Laurentic*, a faster trans-atlantic liner, which would overtake the *Montrose* just before it reached Quebec.

Then followed eight bizarre days. Crippen sat on deck, admiring the 'wonderful invention' of the wireless telegraph, not realizing that he was the subject of the crackling messages. Kendall's daily reports were avidly printed by the *Daily Mail*, whose readers relished every word as the net closed in on the unsuspecting doctor.

It was 08.30 on 31 July when Dew, accompanied by a Canadian policeman, boarded the *Montrose* disguised as a pilot. The ship was in the St Lawrence, and only 16 hours from Quebec. After reporting to Captain Kendall, Dew walked down to the deck and approached his suspect. 'Good morning, Dr Crippen,' he said. 'I am Chief Inspector Dew,' Crippen said only: 'Good morning, Mr Dew.' Ethel, reading in her cabin, screamed, then fainted, when a similar introduction was made. Crippen said later: 'I am not sorry, the anxiety has been too much. It is only fair to say that she knows nothing about it. I never told her anything.' He described Ethel as 'my only comfort for these past three years.'

Dr. Hawley Harvey Crippen, with inset of Ethel,
dressed as a boy

THE WORLD'S MOST INFAMOUS MURDERS

Ivan the Terrible claimed to have seduced 1,000 virgins, killed 1,000 of his own illegitimate offspring, poisoned three of his eight wives, together with their families, and speared to death his own son. Having done away with so many of his own children, he died of syphillis in 1584 leaving only one direct heir, an imbecile called Feodor.

Extradition formalities took less than three weeks, and on 20 August, Dew set sail for England with his celebrated prisoners aboard the liner *SS Megantic*. Dew, who was travelling as Mr Doyle, kept Crippen, now known as Mr Nield, apart from Ethel, though on one evening he did allow the two to gaze silently at each other from their cabin doors, after a request from Crippen. Huge, angry crowds greeted the two at every stage of their rail journey from Liverpool to London. And public feeling was still at fever pitch when their trials began. Crippen was charged with murder, Ethel with being an accessory, and wisely they elected to be tried separately.

The doctor refused to plead guilty, even though he knew he had no credible defence. Seven days before his hearing began, at the Old Bailey on 10 October, the remains found at Hilldrop Crescent were buried at Finchley as those of Cora Crippen. Yet her husband claimed in court that they could have been there when he bought the house in 1905. That argument fell when a buyer for Jones Brothers swore that the pyjama material in which the remains were wrapped was not available until 1908. Two suits in it had been delivered to Crippen in January, 1909.

Crippen had no answer to questions about why he had made no effort to search for his wife after she vanished on 1 February, why no-one had seen her leave the house, why he had then pawned her possessions or given them to Ethel. Bruce Miller, now married and an estate agent in Chicago, said he last saw Cora in 1904, and denied ever having an affair with her.

On the fifth day of the trial, the jury found Crippen guilty after a 27-minute retirement, and Lord Chief Justice Alverstone, who had been scrupulously fair throughout the proceedings, sentenced him to death. Crippen, who had stood up remarkably well to cross-examination, declared: 'I still protest my innocence.'

A curious story, that Crippen had rejected a suggested defence because it would compromise Ethel, began circulating. The line, allegedly suggested by eminent barrister Edward Marshall Hall, was that the doctor had given his nymphomaniac wife hyoscine to calm her demands on him, because he was also making love to Ethel, and that Cora had died through an accidental overdose. Crippen was wise to reject the story, if he did so. For if death was accidental, why go to so much trouble to chop up the body, remove the bones, and to hide the flesh?

All along, he had been anxious to clear Ethel Le Neve's name, and on 25 October the Old Bailey did so after a one-day trial dominated by a brilliant speech by her defence lawyer, F. E. Smith, later Lord Birkenhead. He asked the jury if they could really believe that Crippen would take such care to hide all the traces of the murder, then risk the 'aversion, revulsion and disgust' of a young, nervous woman by telling her: 'This is how I treated the woman who last shared my home, and I invite you to come and share it with me now.' Ethel was found not guilty and discharged.

But she did not desert her lover, and as he waited for execution, he thought only of her, continually proclaiming her innocence, kissing her photograph, and writing touching love letters to her. He also wrote in a statement: 'As I face enternity, I say that Ethel Le Neve has loved me as few women love men . . . surely such love as hers for me will be rewarded.'

The man whose name has become synonymous with murder was hanged in Pentonville Prison on 23 November, 1910, still protesting that he had murdered no-one. His last request was that Ethel's letters and photograph be buried with him. They were. A curious kind of sympathy had grown for the quiet, considerate little man, both among prison staff and those who came into contact with him. F. E. Smith called him 'a brave man and a true lover.' And there were many who agreed with Max Beerbohm Tree's verdict on the day of execution: 'Poor old Crippen.'

Ethel Le Neve slipped quickly into obscurity. Some say she emigrated to Australia, and died there in 1950, others that she went to Canada or America. Another report was that, for 45 years, she ran a tea-room near Bournemouth under an assumed name. And there have been rumours that she wrote her version of the Crippen affair, to be published after her death. But all the theories could be as wide of the mark as the wild legends that have turned her mild-mannered lover into the most monstrous murderer the world has even seen.

The Boston Strangler

ALBERT DESALVO

It was a hot steamy night in June, 1962, when police were called to a run-down apartment building in the centre of Boston. In the bedroom, they found the body of a young woman. Partially clothed, with her limbs arranged in an obscene posture, the woman had been strangled with one of her own stockings.

Although, on that sticky, humid night, the killing seemed only to be a random sex murder, the discovery was the beginning of a reign of terror that was to grip the city and capture the morbid imagination of the nation for more than 18 months. For the murder was the first carried out by one of the most notorious mass murderers of the century . . . 'The Boston Strangler'.

For a year-and-a-half, police sought in vain to unmask the fiend who left his trademark on 11 of the 13 bodies: a single stocking tied tightly around the neck of his victim. Of the two other victims, one was stabbed to death, and another died of a heart attack, allegedly in the arms of the Strangler.

The man behind the mass murders was former US Army boxing champion, Albert DeSalvo. In a twist as bizarre as the killings themselves, DeSalvo was never tried for the Strangler murders, but for an assorted series of robberies and sex attacks on women whom he did not kill.

Although some still express doubt that DeSalvo was the Boston Strangler, the thick-set handyman, who always wore his black hair slicked back and had an obsession for dressing in neat, freshly laundered white shirts, did make a confession to the killings. Facts which only came to light after he was sentenced to life imprisonment seemed to confirm that DeSalvo was indeed the Strangler.

Albert DeSalvo had been in trouble with the law since his childhood, mostly for breaking into homes – a skill that was to be put to terrifying use when he began his killing spree. As a young man he served with the US Army's occupation force in Germany, where he married a local girl, Irmgard. But after having two children, the couple were divorced. He became the Army's middleweight boxing champion, but left the service on his return to America and became a handyman.

DeSalvo had a sexual drive that some doctors described as 'uncontrollable'. Back in his army days, according to one psychiatrist who gave evidence at his trial, his wife constantly complained about his sexual demands. 'She refused

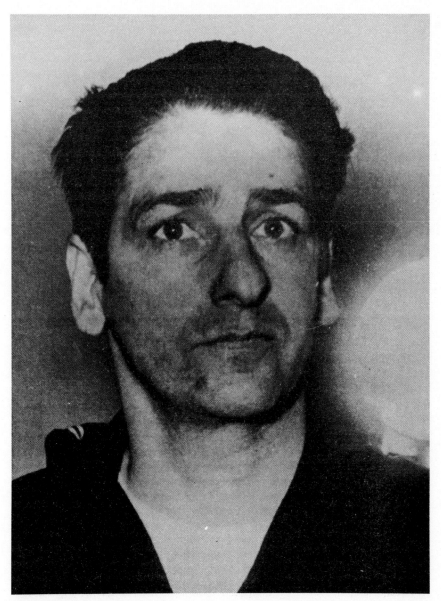

Albert DeSalvo, aged 35

him sex', said Dr James Brussel, 'because he made excessive demands on her. She did not want to submit to his type of kissing which was extensive as far as the body was concerned.'

He added that during his off-duty hours in the army, DeSalvo would engage in wild orgies with the wives of officers who were absent.

'DeSalvo was without doubt, the victim of one of the most crushing sexual drives that psychiatric science has ever encountered', said his lawyer, the famous defence attorney, F. Lee Bailey. 'He was without doubt schizophrenic.'

The wave of killings began in 1962 and, despite the setting up of a special 'Strangler Squad' by law enforcement officers, they continued unabated until 1964. In each case, the women who fell victim to the Strangler were killed in their own homes. DeSalvo gained access to their apartments by posing as a delivery man or by claiming he had been sent by the superintendent of the building to check a leaking waterpipe.

Many of the Strangler's victims were sexually molested, which was in keeping with DeSalvo's insatiable sex drive. They were nearly all undressed, and their bodies arranged in obscene poses.

As the murders continued unabated, so the fear and panic among the citizens of Boston increased. Few took to the streets by themselves at night. Husbands going away on business left their wives loaded guns at their bedsides. Police patrols reached an unprecedented level. But despite the rising death toll, and the almost daily arrest – and release – of possible suspects, Albert DeSalvo, then 32 was never once interviewed by police. He should have been a prime target for investigation . . . having only just been released from prison after serving six months for sex offences. He had posed as an agent for a top modelling agency, and persuaded young women to allow him to take their measurements. But it was just an excuse to molest them, and he was arrested for what became known as the 'Measuring Man' attacks.

Then in 1964 he was arrested for the 'Green Man' attacks. He was nick-named the 'Green Man' because of his love for green trousers, which he always wore when he broke into the homes of single women. He would strip his victims at knife-point and kiss them all over, before making his escape. A description given by one of the victims, however, was matched by a detective, as being an exact description of the 'Measuring Man', and DeSalvo was brought in.

After his arrest, he was taken to the Bridgewater Mental Institute in Massachusetts, where the terrible truth was to come out.

At his trial for the 'Green Man' offences, psychiatrist Robert Mezer stunned the court when he revealed that DeSalvo had admitted to him in hospital that he was the Strangler. He said that during an interview at Bridgewater, DeSalvo had confessed he strangled 13 women. 'He went into details about some of them, telling me some of the intimate acts he had committed.'

But by Massachusetts' law no doctor who takes information from a suspect in a case can give it as evidence in a courtroom, so the full story never came out at DeSalvo's trial. However, there is little doubt in the minds of most experts that DeSalvo was the Boston Strangler. Probably the most telling revelations came from his defence lawyer, F. Lee Bailey, in his book, *The Defence Never Rests*. He explained that that DeSalvo had made another confession, this time to doctors and law enforcement officers, in a dramatic meeting in July 1965. But because of a special deal between the police and the defence, the evidence was never used.

'I wanted DeSalvo studied by experts, and the authorities wanted to be able to end their investigation. In both cases, DeSalvo's identification as the Boston Strangler had to be irrefutably established. That was only possible if the police interviewed him and matched his memory against the myriad of details of the 13 murders.'

After striking the bargain that the conversations with DeSalvo would not be used in court, the meeting took place at the Bridgewater Mental Institute. It was supposed to take only 15 minutes. Instead it took more than five hours, as more and more damning evidence that DeSalvo was the Strangler was to emerge. He revealed information about the victims that only the real murderer could possibly have known. He said there was a notebook under the bed of victim number eight, brunette Beverly Samans. He was also able to draw floor plans of the apartments of his victims, and could give clear descriptions of the furnishings and decoration.

These and other details added up to more than 50 hours of tapes made at subsequent interviews with DeSalvo and more than 2000 pages of transcript. All details were checked and all were correct.

But the dramatic details that could have convicted DeSalvo as the Boston Strangler were never fully revealed until after his trial for the other offences. And the only man who could know with certainty whether he had killed 13 women, Albert DeSalvo, is now silenced for ever. In 1973, six years after he was sent to Walpole State Prison, in Massachusetts, DeSalvo was stabbed to death by three other inmates, in a row over drugs.

The Lonely Hearts Killers

RAYMOND FERNANDEZ AND MARTHA BECK

Raymond Fernandez and Martha Beck were two social misfits whose crimes outraged the society that had scorned them. Both had at one stage led almost normal, useful lives, but fate had played cruel tricks on them. After they teamed up in 1947, it was they who played the cruel tricks. And they paid for them with their lives.

Fernandez, born in Hawaii of Spanish parents, moved to Spain in the 1930s and married a Spanish woman. After serving in Franco's forces during the Civil War, and gaining the reputation of a war hero, he worked with distinction for British intelligence in the Gibraltar docks. In 1945, he sailed for America, working his passage on an oil tanker. During the voyage, a hatch cover fell on his head. He recovered in hospital at Curaçao, but his personality had changed radically. He became a cunning, ruthless swindler, convinced that he had supernatural powers over women, and determined to use them to the utmost.

He began advertizing in lonely hearts magazines, and fleecing the gullible people who answered his pleas. By 1947 he had claimed more than 100 victims. He was just back from Spain, where his latest dupe had died mysteriously during their holiday, when he decided to follow up an intriguing letter from a woman in Florida with a personal visit.

Martha Beck's name had been forwarded to the lonely hearts club as a joke by one of her friends. Martha was an outsize woman of 280lb whose bulk and sexuality constantly made her a figure of fun to others. At 13 she had been raped by her own brother, who continued the incestuous relationship until she complained to her mother. For reasons which Martha never understood, she was blamed for the sordid affair, and forced to live a cloistered existence which deprived her of normal relationships as a teenager.

She became a nurse, moving to California and an army hospital. But the scandals of her nymphomaniac sex life forced her to return east, where she became superintendent of a home for crippled children at Pensacola, Florida. There she met Fernandez, who was using his business name, Charles Martin.

A torrid affair quickly began, Fernandez introducing Martha to new perversions which satisfied her sexually for the first time in her life. She gave up her job and left behind her two children, one illegitimate, the other the product

THE LONELY HEARTS KILLERS

Raymond Fernandez (second from left) and Martha Beck examined at court in Michigan

of a disastrous marriage, to follow Fernandez. When he explained his line of business, she agreed to become his accomplice, posing as his sister. But she loved him too much to allow him a free hand. He could woo and wed women – but she would not allow him to consummate the marriages.

Such jealousy hampered the romantic con-man. The first joint effort resulted in the victim claiming back her car and $500, and refusing to sign over her insurance policies. The ill-starred lovers moved on to Cook County, Illinois, and Fernandez married Myrtle Young in August 1948. But again there were violent rows when the bride expected to sleep alone with her husband, and Martha refused to allow it. Myrtle was given an overdose of barbiturates, and put on a bus to Little Rock, Arkansas. She collapsed and died there. Fernandez and Beck made $4,000 and gained a car.

In Albany, New York, that December, Fernandez charmed a naive widow, Janet Fay, 66, into signing over all her assets and her $6,000 insurance policy to him. Then she was strangled and battered to death with a hammer. The body was stuffed into a trunk, and the couple took it with them to New York City, where they rented a house in Queens, and buried the makeshift coffin under cement in the cellar.

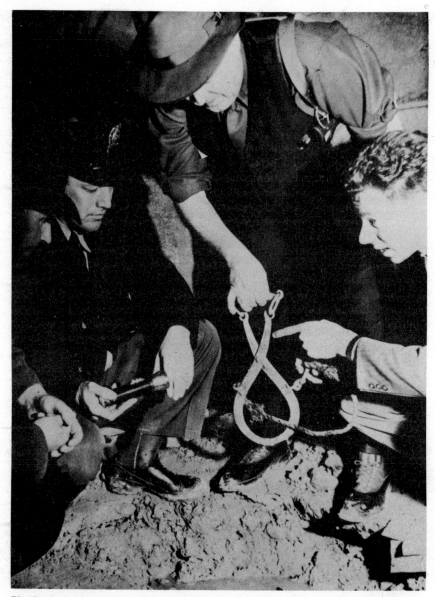

Bloodstained tongs discovered in the cellar where Mrs Downing and daughter were found

THE LONELY HEARTS KILLERS

The following year Fernandez and Beck were in Grand Rapids, Michigan, trying to fleece a 28-year-old widow called Delphine Downing. Once again, Martha reacted angrily when Fernandez started sleeping with her. Then Delphine saw her husband without his toupe, and threatened to leave him. Fernandez and Beck were out at the cinema, found the two bodies, and arrested Rainelle. Both bodies were cemented into the cellar floor, and curious neighbours were told that Delphine and her daughter were away on holiday.

But suspicious relatives called the police. They searched the house while Fernandez and beck were out at the cinema, found the two bodies, and arrested the couple on their return. A curious tug-of-war between two states now began. Michigan did not have the death penalty, but New York did. The murder of Janet Fay had been discovered, and New York asked for the couple to be sent there for trial. Public fury at the couple's evil exploits played some part in New York getting its way.

Fernandez and Beck were charged with three murders, and suspected of 17 more, including that of Myrtle Young. The trial began in July 1949, and lasted 44 days. Press coverage of the proceedings was unprecendented in its hatred and intolerance, and every intimate detail of the sordid sex life of the couple created sensational headlines. Crowds flocked to the courtroom to catch a glimpse of the 'monster' and his 'overweight ogress'.

The verdict was never in doubt. Fernandez and Beck were found guilty of first-degree murder, and sentenced to death on 29 August. Their appeals were dismissed and on 8 March, 1951, they went to the electric chair at Sing-Sing Prison.

Two hours before the execution, Fernandez sent Martha a message of love. She said: 'Now that I know Raymond loves me, I can go to my death bursting with joy.' But there was nothing joyful about the death. Newspapers gleefully reported the struggle to fit her huge bulk into the chair, and the prolonged writhing as the electric shocks struggled to have an impact through her flabby body. Such was public distaste for the Lonely Hearts Killers that more people laughed at that last ordeal than felt pity for its victim.

The Killer Clown

JOHN WAYNE GACY

When they christened him with the name of their favourite film star, John Wayne Gacy's parents had high hopes that their little boy would one day become famous. In a way they saw their dreams realized – although not quite as wished.

John Wayne Gacy today is a name that conjures up revulsion among millions of Americans. He is one of the country's most sadistic and prolific mass murderers, and known as the Killer Clown. When he was finally tracked down and tackled by the Chicago police in 1978, Gacy readily admitted to murdering no fewer than 33 young men and boys. Before strangling and stabbing them to death, he had brutally raped them.

Gacy was a fat, lonely homosexual with an insatiable sexual appetite. He longed to be loved by the neighbours who regarded him as 'a wierdo'. And he had aspirations of becoming somebody in local politics. To that end, he began a deliberate campaign to win over the local populace in the Chicago suburb of Norwood Park Township. A friend with connections in the Democratic Party showed him how: he would have to become a local benefactor with particular emphasis on the neighbourhood children.

Gacy set about this task with gusto. He designed three clown outfits himself, then set about creating a character. Very soon he was a local celebrity as Pogo the Clown, performing in the streets, at children's parties and other functions. He was so successful that President Carter's wife Rosalynn posed with him for a photograph, then sent him an autographed copy. He treasured that.

But while 38-year-old Gacy clowned for the kids and posed for posterity, the Chicago police were baffled by the mysterious disappearance of a number of local youths. On their files were also several missing persons from other states.

It took the police six years to nail Gacy. When they did, they met with a torrent of abuse from residents of Northwood Park for the appalling record of overlooked clues and bungled detective work. Had they been more efficient, people argued, at least some of the Killer Clown's victims might have lived. In fact, on four occasions between 1972 and 1978, Gacy's name had appeared on police files as a suspect in the missing persons cases. He had also been convicted twice for sex assaults on young men.

Interviewed at police headquarters, Gacy drew a detailed map of his

Above: Police search John Wayne Gacy's home for more bodies

Right: John Wayne Gacy, convicted of killing 33 men and boys

property, pinpointing the location of 28 of the bodies. After raping and killing his victims, he had methodically buried them in the extensive, landscaped garden of his neat and modern ranch house. The bodies of five other boys had been thrown into the Des Plaines river, near his home.

Gacy had been heavily influenced by his mother since childhood. His older sister also seemed to dominate him. He was a weak-willed man who carried his resentment towards women with him through later life. Nevertheless, he was determined to succeed in business. And that much he did. From humble beginnings, he built up a construction business that flourished.

Gacy took advantage of the rising unemployment in Chicago and offered jobs to young unskilled men who stood the least chance of finding employment. His local lads were all under 20 and receiving unemployment benefit. Others he picked up from the Greyhound Bus station in Chicago: these were often drifters heading for California hoping to find their pot of gold. Instead they found death.

'I wanted to give these young people a chance' he told police during questioning. 'Young people always get a raw deal. But if you give them responsibility they rise to the occasion. They're hard workers and proud of their work.'

Gacy's teenage workforce were well-paid and happy. As the contracts continued to pour in, he needed more labourers. At the end of a hard day – for he put in many hours himself – Gacy would get into his Oldsmobile and head for the Greyhound Station, looking for more employees among the itinerants. He always found somebody.

He had been married in 1967 and again five years after that. His first wife, who divorced him in 1969, bore him two children. She said of him. 'He was a likeable salesman who could charm anything right out of you.' Wife number two, Carole Hoff, said her husband 'started bringing home a lot of pictures of

---

Unrepentant sex assaulter, robber and murderer Carl Panzram could not wait to be hanged. He told his executioner at Fort Leavenworth, Texas, in 1930: 'While you're fooling around, I could hang a dozen men.' Panzram's life was one of insatiable hatred. 'I hate the whole darn race, including myself,' he said. And he had proved it by murdering more than 21 people and committing thousands of burglaries.

Sentenced to 25 years at Fort Leavenworth, he threatened to kill the first man who angered him. He carried out the threat shortly afterwards by murdering a prison laundry worker. When sentenced to be executed, he said he looked forward to it as 'a pleasure and a great relief'.

THE KILLER CLOWN

> John Wesley Hardin started out as a Texas Sunday school teacher and ended up a cold, calculating killer. From the age of 15, when he murdered a negro slave and shot two soldiers who tried to catch him, he continued his rampage of slaughter until his death in 1895 at the age of 42. He was reputed to have murdered between 24 and 40 people, most of them black.

naked men' just before they separated. They were divorced in 1976. Both his wives described him as 'mysterious' and said he had been a normal husband for the first few months of marriage, but then began staying out at night in his car. He beat his wives.

Where did Gacy go? Later it emerged that he would frequent 'Bughouse Square', a notorious corner of Chicago populated at night by legions of young homosexuals and male prostitutes. He picked up young men and they, like the itinerants and the local boys who worked for his building company, were among the dead found later by police.

All this time, Gacy was winning friends and influencing people with his Pogo The Clown antics. He made hefty contributions to the Democratic Party, which he supported wholeheartedly. In the three years before his capture, Gacy funded and organized an annual political summer fete with beer, hamburgers and music and attended by five hundred local dignitaries and business bigwigs. The proceeds went to President Carter's re-election fund, and for his efforts he was lauded by the White House.

A pure coincidence led to his arrest. One of Gacy's political contacts during this time had known one of the victims, and harried police into mounting an extraordinarily intensive search for the missing youngster. Once again, as had happened on several occasions years before, the trail seemed to lead to Gacy. Police raided his luxury ranch house in December 1978. They placed Gacy under arrest and a team of forensic experts moved in, combing the place for clues.

As the horrified neighbours watched, police systematically dug up the garden. By the third day, the remains of 28 different bodies had been unearthed. Gacy had at first denied murdering anyone, but gradually admitted the first few, then finally drew a detailed map of his garden for police. The five remaining corpses were fished out of the Des Plaines river by police frogmen in a massive dredging operation.

Details of Gacy's *modus operandi* emerged over the ensuing months. Since boyhood, he had had a fixation for police matters. He loved to play policeman, and owned guns and other paraphernalia, including handcuffs. When he got a

> **A German tailor was hanged for Britain's first murder on a train, mainly because he picked up the wrong hat at the scene of the crime. Bank clerk Thomas Briggs, 70, was found dead on the railway line between Hackney Wick and Bow, London, on 9 July, 1864. His gold watch and hat were among the items missing, and a silk hat found near the body was identified as belonging to Franz Muller, 25. Police discovered that Muller had set sail for America on the SS *Victoria*. They took a faster liner, and were waiting to arrest him at New York. Despite a personal plea to Queen Victoria from the Prussian king, Muller was hanged on 14 November, 1864.**

young man back to his house he would show the unsuspecting fellow the 'handcuff trick', assuring him that he would be released after only a few seconds. Instead, of course, once the victim was in Gacy's power, he would become the subject of a wild homosexual rape. Instead of learning, as Gacy had promised, how to get free from the handcuffs, the victim would hear Gacy say: 'The way to get out of these handcuffs is to have the key. That's the real trick.'

The handcuff trick was quickly followed by the 'rope trick' and this always spelled the end for the victim. Gacy would throw a piece of cord around the victim's neck, and tie two knots in it. Then he would push a piece of wood through the loop and slowly turn. Within seconds the victim was unconscious: a few seconds more and he was dead.

At his trial in 1979, Chicago District Attorney William Kunkle described him as a sick man who methodically planned and executed his many murders. Kunkle asked for the death penalty; the State of Illinois was then debating whether to reintroduce execution for certain types of murder.

Defence attorney Sam Amirante pleaded that Cary was insane at the time he committed the murders. But there had been so many, and over such a long period of time that Gacy was convicted and given life imprisonment.

The Vampire Killer

JOHN HAIGH

Donald McSwann entered a den of death when he followed his friend John Haigh into his basement workshop. McSwann operated a pinball arcade in London where Haigh sometimes worked as a mechanic. Haigh boasted about his workshop and it was, indeed, a basement to be proud of. There was equipment for every kind of craftsman . . . for the carpenter, the welder, the sheet metal worker – and the murderer.

McSwann stared at the 40-gallon vat of sulphuric acid in one corner. His curiosity drove him to ask about the need for such a strange array of equipment. His questions were never answered. Crouching behind him, Haigh viciously swung a hammer in a deadly arc . . . and he had slaughtered his first victim.

According to Haigh, when he later confessed to the crime, he drank some of McSwann's blood. Then he spent the night methodically dismembering his body and feeding it into the vat. The sulphuric acid bubbled and smoked, occasionally forcing him to escape outdoors for a breath of fresh air. By the next afternoon, McSwann's remains had dissolved into a mass of sludge. Haigh disposed of it, bucket by bucket, sloshing the ghastly residue into a basement manhole connected to the sewer system.

It was September 1944 and no one thought anything of McSwann's disappearance. Haigh's murder-for-profit scheme was succeeding to perfection.

He assured McSwann's aging parents that their son was hiding out in Scotland until the end of the war. Haigh even went to Scotland once a week to post a letter to them signing McSwann's name.

In between the trips, he ran the pinball arcade business that had belonged to his victim. Wartime crowds poured into the arcade and Haigh was taking in money hand over fist. But it was still not enough to buy the lifestyle he wanted, and greed drove him to his next murder for profit.

His victims were to be McSwann's parents. He wrote to them, again forging their son's name, and begged them to meet him at the home of his dear friend, John Haigh.

On the night of 10 July, 1945, Haigh bludgeoned them to death in his workshop. Afterwards he dissolved their bodies in the vat of acid and poured the reeking sludge down the drain.

Using forged documents Haigh helped himself to the entire estate – five

THE WORLD'S MOST INFAMOUS MURDERS

The kidnapping of the 20-month-old son of world-famous aviator Charles Lindbergh scandalized America on 1 March, 1932. The boy was taken from his luxury New Jersey home, and the anguished father was desperate enough to pay a $75,000 ransom, but there was no child in return. On 12 May the boy's body was found in a shallow grave near Lindbergh's home. But it was September before the killer was found – he handed in a note from the ransom money at a petrol station, and was traced through his car registration number. Bruno Hauptmann, 36, a former German soldier who had entered America illegally in 1923, went to the electric chair at Trenton, New Jersey, on 3 April, 1936.

houses and a fortune in securities and later transferred it to his own name.

Because of his inveterate gambling, self-indulgence and a string of bad investments, he was broke again by February 1948. He decided to invite a young married couple, Rosalie and Dr Archie Henderson, to look at his new workshop at Crawley, south of London. Both went into the acid bath.

Although the Henderson's estate had been profitably disposed of in 1949 Haigh found that he needed one more victim. Still convinced he was living a charmed life, he chose this one with little caution.

She was Mrs Olive Durand-Deacon, a 69-year-old widow whose husband had left her £40,000. She lived at the same London residential hotel as Haigh, who had not paid his bills for months and who was desperate for money.

Mrs Durand-Deacon believed that, apart from having a private income, Haigh had made money by patenting inventions. She put to him an idea for false plastic fingernails. Haigh showed interest, invited her to visit his Crawley workshop and in February 1949 drove her down there.

What happened next was described by Haigh in a statement he made to police and which was read at his trial:

> She was inveigled by me into going to Crawley in view of her interest in artificial fingernails. Having taken her into the storeroom, I shot her through the back of the head while she was examining some materials.
>
> Then I went out to the car and fetched a drinking glass and made an incision – I think with a penknife – in the side of her throat. I collected a glass of blood, which I drank.
>
> I removed her coat and jewellery (rings, necklace, earrings and crucifix) and put her in a 45-gallon tank.
>
> Before I put her handbag in the tank, I took from it about 30 shillings and a fountain pen. I then filled the tank with sulphuric acid, by means of a stirrup-pump. I then left it to react.

THE VAMPIRE KILLER

As an afterthrought, Haid added: 'I should have said that, in between having her in the tank and pumping in the acid, I went round to the Ancient Prior's [a local teashop] for a cup of tea.'

It took some days and two further trips to Crawley to check on the acid tank before Mrs Durand-Deacon's body appeared to have been entirely dissolved. Meantime, the police had questioned her fellow guests at the hotel, including Haigh.

The killer's glib, over-helpful manner made one detective particularly suspicious and he checked on the 39-year-old suspects background. He unearthed a prison record for minor frauds and arrested Haigh. The murderer confessed, but claimed that he could never be proven guilty because police could never find any of his victims' remains.

He was wrong. Forensic scientists examined the foul sludge that had been emptied from the tank onto the ground in the yard of the Crawley workshop. They were able to identify a gallstone, part of a foot, remains of a handbag and an almost complete set of false teeth. These were shown to Mrs Durand-Deacon's dentist, who confirmed that they had belonged to the trusting widow.

In court Haigh's lawyers claimed that the killer was insane. They pointed to a strict and unhappy childhood – his parents belonged to the Plymouth Brethren – and to his claimed habit of drinking his victims' blood. But although the British press labelled him The Vampire Killer, the judge and jury failed to accept this bloody trait as evidence of insanity. After a trial of only two days, he was found guilty of murdering Mrs Durand-Deacon and sentenced to death. Asked if he had anything to say, Haigh replied airily: 'Nothing at all.'

On 6 August, 1949, he was hanged at Wandsworth Prison.

The A6 Lay-By Murder

JAMES HANRATTY

The A6 murder has led to more controversy than almost any other killing in Britain. An illiterate, feeble-minded petty criminal called James Hanratty was hanged for it after the longest murder trial in English legal history. Ever since, an extensive and distinguished lobby of authors has campaigned to persuade the public that British justice executed the wrong man.

At dusk on 22 August, 1961, two scientific workers at the Road Research Laboratory in Slough, Buckinghamshire, were cuddling in the front seat of a grey Morris Minor saloon in a cornfield at Dorney Reach, beside the river Thames between Windsor and Maidenhead. Michael Gregsten was 38, a married man with two children. Valerie Storie was an attractive, single 23-year-old who had been his mistress for three years.

They were interrupted by a tap on the driver's side window. Gregsten wound down the window, and the man standing there pointed a gun at him. The terrified couple thought it was a hold-up. They offered the man their money, watches, even the car. He sat in the back seat, warning them not to look at him, toying with the gun. He told them he was on the run, and that every policeman in Britain was on the look-out for him. But he seemed undecided about what he was going to do.

Finally, at about 23.30, he ordered Gregsten to start driving. There followed a bizarre 30-mile drive through the northern suburbs of London, Slough, Hayes and Stanmore, broken only by stops to buy petrol and cigarettes. Gregsten, nervous already, was put further on edge by the back-seat driving of his captor, issuing instructions about the route and urging care at blackspots. They turned on to the A5 towards St Albans, Gregsten occasionally flashing his reversing lights to try to attract attention, and keeping an eye out for policemen, so he could stage a crash. He saw none.

On the A6, between St Albans and Luton, the gunman ordered Gregsten to pull into a lay-by. He said he wanted 'a kip', and made an attempt to tie Miss Storie to a door handle. He asked Gregsten to hand him a duffle bag, but as the driver reached for it, he was shot twice in the head. 'He moved too quick, he frightened me,' the gunman said as the girl screamed: 'You bastard.'

As blood flowed from her lover's wounds, Miss Storie was forced into the back

74

seat, ordered to remove some of her clothes, then raped. The man then made Miss Storie pull Gregsten's body from the car to the edge of the concrete lay-by. She sat beside the body, too stunned to cry, while the man continued to dither about what to do next.

Eventually, Miss Storie gave him a £1 note if he would leave quickly. He took it, and seemed to be going. But as he approached the car, he unexpectedly turned, and pumped five bullets at the girl. One pierced her neck, close to the spinal cord. She lay still, pretending to be dead, as he strode over to inspect his work. Convinced he had eliminated the only witness to his earlier killing, he drove off.

Passing drivers failed to hear Miss Storie's screams. She took off and waved her petticoat, but no-one saw it in the dark. At last she passed out, and was found at around 06.30 by a teenager arriving for a traffic census. She recovered consciousness in hospital, and began giving waiting police officers extremely detailed descriptions of all that had happened. Her wounds had paralyzed her, consigning her to life in a wheelchair, but her mind was unaffected.

Two identikit pictures were issued, based on her descriptions, and those of witnesses who saw Gregsten's car being driven before it was abandoned in Ilford, Essex. Police were following a confusing trail of clues. At first they suspected Peter Louis Alphon. Two .38 bullets were found in the hotel room at the Vienna Hotel, Maida Vale, where he spent the night after the murder. Ballistics experts matched them with those that had killed Gregsten. But when Alphon was put in an identity parade, Valerie Storie failed to pick him out. She selected one of the stooges who could not possibly have been the murderer. Alphon did not match the identikit descriptions, nor did James Hanratty. And the police did not suspect him because he was known to them only as a petty and none-too-successful villain. But then he seemed to go out of his way to attract attention.

Police were already puzzled by anonymous calls to the hospital where Valerie Storie was recovering, threatening her life. They moved her to a fresh

---

Twice-convicted murderer Walter Graham Rowland almost cheated the gallows before his luck finally ran out. Rowland strangled his two-year-old daughter and killed a 40-year-old prostitute, Olive Balchin, with a hammer. He was convicted of the child's murder, sentenced, then reprieved.

It seemed as if he would escape the gallows a second time when a prisoner in Walton Jail, Liverpool, confessed to the prostitute's murder. But the statement was found to be false and Rowland was hanged in 1947.

THE WORLD'S MOST INFAMOUS MURDERS

Bugsy Siegel was a cunning killer who mixed with the Hollywood stars and thought there was nothing more important than a touch of class. From the squalor of Brooklyn, he graduated to racketeering and bootlegging and became New York's top hit man. In 1945 he borrowed $3 million to build a hotel in Las Vegas. Siegel refused to repay the money and was murdered in his home by an unknown gunman in 1947.

bed every night, and reinforced the guard on her. Then Hanratty phoned Detective Superintendent Acott, the man in charge of the hunt, saying he was anxious about being suspected for the A6 murder, and denying his involvement. Since the call was completely unsolicited, Hanratty immediately became a prime suspect.

Police discovered that he had asked an associate, Charles France, whether the back seat of a London bus was a good place to hide a gun. Hanratty was known to have acquired a .38 Enfield revolver earlier in the year. A similar gun was found behind the rear seat on the top deck of a No 36 bus. Police also discovered that Hanratty had booked into the Vienna Hotel the night before Alphon, staying in the same room as J. Ryan. And Gregsten's widow named him as the likely killer of her husband, though many wondered how she could possibly know.

Hanratty was arrested in Blackpool on 9 October and put in an identity parade. Valerie Storie again failed to pick him out, though she had now mentioned piercing blue eyes in her description of the killer. Hanratty had such eyes. She then asked each of the line-up to say the words the murderer had used several times: 'Be quiet, will you, I am thinking.' Hanratty always pronounced the last work 'finking'. And it was then that Miss Storie indentified him.

The trail began on 22 January, 1962. The police were given a hard time by the defence, who accused them of concentrating on implicating Hanratty instead of hunting down the truth. Much was also made of Miss Storie's identity parade failures, and the changes in her description of the killer.

But the defence was not helped by Hanratty himself. Though he pleaded not guilty, he was cocky and insolent throughout. A fellow prisoner who had been in custody with Hanratty swore that he had confessed to the killing and gave details of it known only to police and Miss Storie. Hanratty claimed that at the time of the murder he was in Liverpool with friends. But he refused to name them, saying to do so would break their trust in him. Then, inexplicably, he changed his alibi, and said he was in Rhyl, North Wales. Again he could not prove it.

There were enough doubts about both the prosecution and defence cases to keep the jury out for nine-and-a-half hours on 11 February. Once they returned for guidance from the judge. Then they filed back to court to return a verdict of guilty. He said only: 'I an innocent.' Every appeal was rejected. Hanratty, aged 25, was hanged at Bedford Prison on 4 April, 1962.

But even today, there are those who say there was too much 'reasonable doubt' about the affair to condemn any man. Peter Alphon made a series of sensational confessions to newspapers, saying Hanratty's conviction was contrived. Later, however, he withdrew them all. Charles France, Hanratty's friend, who had given evidence about the gun against him in court, hanged himself, leaving a note about the case. But it was not read at the inquest on the grounds that it was not in the public interest. Witnesses then came forward to claim that they had seen Hanratty in Rhyl on the night of the murder.

Books by Louis Blom-Cooper, Paul Foot and Ludovic Kennedy all helped to make Hanratty the greatest *cause célèbre* since Timothy Evans, another none-too-bright man executed for murder. But whereas Evans was condemned by Christie's evil lies, and was posthumously pardoned, Hanratty had virtually condemned himself by changing his alibi in court. And for everyone who claimed he was unjustly hanged, there were others who agreed with Detective-Superintendent Acott that Hanratty was 'one of the worst types of killers in recent years.'

The Mass-Murderer of Hanover

FRITZ HAARMANN

Wild terror, more akin to the Middle Ages than the 20th century, swept the north German town of Hanover in the spring of 1924. In winding alleys beneath the gabled roofs of the old quarter, people whispered that a werewolf was at large, devouring anyone foolish enough to venture out after dark. Some said children were being butchered in cellars. Police doctors were inundated with strange-tasting meat brought in by housewives who feared it was human flesh. The authorities dismissed the alarm as 'mass hysteria'. And they blamed a prank by medical students when children found the first of many human skulls beside the river Leine on 17 May.

The authorities were as wrong as the panic-stricken public. But the truth, when it emerged later that year, was just as macabre as the people's wildest fears. It ended in execution for a 45-year-old mass murderer called Fritz Haarmann, the jailing of his 25-year-old partner in crime – and a national scandal.

Haarmann had been a wandering vagrant, hawker and pilferer for most of his life. He worshipped his mother – an invalid after his birth in Hanover on 25 October, 1879 – and hated his father, a morose, miserly locomotive stoker known to all as Sulky Olle. When Fritz's bitterness spilled into violence, his father tried to get him committed to an asylum. But doctors decided that, though the boy was incurably feeble-minded, there were no grounds to commit him.

He roamed the country, a popular figure with the underworld and the police of many cities. Fellow petty crooks regarded him as fat and stupid, but kind, always ready to offer help, money and advice to those worse off than himself. The police liked him because he always came quietly when arrested, laughing and joking with them. He was always a model prisoner, accepting and even enjoying jail discipline. He served time for picking pockets, petty thieving and indecent behaviour with small children.

In 1918, Haarmann emerged from a five-year sentence for theft and fraud to find post-war Germany in chaos. Law and order had broken down, and profiteers, swindlers and crooks reigned supreme in the anarchy. These were the people Harrmann understood. He returned to Hanover, spending most of his time among the con-men and dubious traders at the straggling markets outside the central railway station. He became obsessed with the people inside the station – refugees from all over Germany, human flotsam without jobs or money, homes or hopes, who cowered round stoves by day, and huddled on platform benches at night.

Haarmann knew he could make a living in this twilight world, but, as he grew more and more acustomed to it, he realized there were other opportunities for him. Among the down-and-outs were many teenage boys, some no more than 12 years old. They had run away from home, often unable to cope with life there once their stern fathers returned from the war after years away. Haarmann turned on his charm with them, listening to their grievances, offering them advice, winning their confidence. In a country where everyone was carefully documented, he had discovered a constant flow of people nobody could trace. They could disappear for ever, and their parents and the police would be none the wiser.

Haarmann took lodgings at 27, Cellarstrasse, and set up in business as a meat-hawker and seller of secondhand clothes. He could haggle with the best of the market traders, and his business soon prospered. Housewives quickly learned that his prices were lower than anyone else's, and that his stock was always plentiful and varied. But he still spent his evenings with the boys at the station, laughing and joking with them, handing round chocolates and cigarettes, greeting hungry, forlorn new arrivals with the cheery offer of a meal and a mattress for the night.

Within weeks, Haarmann was such a familiar face there that welfare workers considered him almost as one of them. And the police decided to use his services, too. They needed spies in the underworld to try to stem the growing crime and corruption, and rewarded their 'narks' by turning a blind eye to their activities, legal and otherwise. Haarmann was delighted to help. Using the intimate knowledge of crooks he had gained over the years, he quickly earned the nickname of 'Detective' by reporting crimes, hiding places and plots. In return, the police did not pry into his business. And they were loathe to inquire too closely in September, 1918, when the parents of 17-year-old Friedel Rothe reported him missing after he was seen with Haarmann in a billiards room. It took the threat of force to persuade the officers to visit Haarmann's rooms, and their search was merely cursory.

Six years later, Haarmann was to brag at his trial: 'When the police examined my room, the head of the boy Friedel was lying wrapped in newspaper behind the oven.' For the truth was that the 'Detective' was not the bluff, genial do-gooder he seemed. The wretched youngsters he befriended were taken to his home for a good meal, often sexually assaulted, then killed in the most savage fashion – a bite at the throat. The bodies were then dismembered, the meat being sold, the skull and bones being disposed of in the river Leine.

THE WORLD'S MOST INFAMOUS MURDERS

That narrow escape in 1918 did not make Haarmann more cautious. If anything he became bolder as the police relied more and more on his information. And in September 1919 he met the accomplice who was to incite him to more murders. Hans Grans was then 20, and himself a runaway from home. Slim, graceful, cynical and emotionless, the librarian's son soon established ascendancy over his social inferior, taunting him with insults and sarcasm. And he began to order the killing of selected victims, often merely because he coveted their clothing.

The two men moved to rooms in Neuestrasse, then into an alley called Rothe Reihe (Red Row), almost on the banks of the Leine. Neighbours noted that a constant stream of young boys went into the apartment, but that none ever seemed to come out. They overheard sounds of chopping and splashing. Occasionally police brought the grief-stricken parents of missing boys to the rooms. They had heard that their sons had last been seen with the 'Detective'. Somehow, they always left satisfied that Haarmann had nothing to do with the disappearances.

One morning, a neighbour met Harrmann on the stairs. As he stopped to gossip and joke with her, a paper covering the bucket he was carrying slipped slightly, and she saw that the bucket was full of blood. But she said nothing to the authorities. After all, Haarmann had to hack carcasses of meat as part of his trade. Another neighbour once heard him chopping in his room, and asked: 'Am I going to get a bit.' He chuckled: 'No, next time.' She also saw a young boy lying very still on Haarmann's bed, but was told: 'Don't wake him, he's asleep.' A customer took a piece of meat bought from Haarmann to the police doctor because she was suspicious of its taste. She was told it was pork.

By 1923, Haarmann had made himself indispensible to the police. Not only was he still informing on criminals, he had set up a detective agency in partnership with a highly-placed police official, and was also recruiting for the Black *Reichswehr*, a secret organization working against French occupation of the Ruhr. He was so sure of police protection that he was taking enormous risks, selling the clothes of victims only a day or two after murdering them. One woman bought a pair of socks from him for her son, and found two spots of blood on them. She threw them away. A man spotted Grans wearing a suit that, days earlier, had belonged to a boy at the railway station.

But pressure was building up on the police. Newspapers had noted that large numbers of youths from all over north Germany had arrived in Hanover, then vanished. One paper claimed that 600 had disappeared in just one year. Hanover was acquiring a sinister reputation. The published fears brought out into the open suspicions many had been prepared to keep to themselves. The discovery of the skull by the river Leine in May 1924 was the final straw.

Now the police had to deal not with the occasional distraught parent, but with outraged public opinion. Another skull was discovered by the river on 29 May – a small skull, about the size of a young boy. Two more were unearthed on 13 June. A police spokesman claimed they could have been swept down-river from Alfeld, where hurried burials were taking place due to a typhus outbreak. But the explanation was not accepted by the frightened public. They believed a monster was preying on their town – and many were convinced that he lived in Rothe Reihe. Faced with a mounting tide of witnesses pointing the finger at Haarmann, the chief of police decided to act.

Haarmann still had powerful friends, impressed by the help he was giving the authorities. So the police chief moved cautiously. He brought in two detectives from Berlin, instructing them to watch Haarmann's movements at the station. On the evening of 22 June, 1924, he approached a boy called Fromm who objected to his attentions. They began to quarrel, then fight, and the detectives moved in to arrest them both.

With Haarmann safe at headquarters, a police squad swooped on his rooms. The walls were splashed with blood, and there were heaps of clothing and personal possessions. Haarmann protested that since he was both a meat trader and a clothes salesman, such findings were not unexpected. Then the mother of a missing boy recognized his coat – being worn by the son of Haarmann's landlady.

The game was up, and Haarmann knew it. He broke down and confessed to several murders, accusing Grans of instigating and assisting in many of them. Grans was immediately arrested. Meanwhile, more and more human remains were being discovered beside the River Leine. Boys playing in a meadow found a sack packed with them on 24 July. When dredgers probed the black ooze of the riverbed, watched by thousands lining the banks, they brought to the surface 500 bones.

Haarmann and Grans were tried at Hanover Assizes on 4 December, accused of killing 27 boys aged between 12 and 18. Haarmann was allowed to interrupt the proceedings almost as he pleased, and his grisly attempts at humour only added to the horror as the full story of his butchery unfolded.

'You're doing fine,' he shouted when the prosecution finished their opening speech. When one witness took his time pondering a question, Haarmann yelled: 'Come on, old chap. You must tell us all you know. We are here to get the truth.' Impatient when a distressed mother broke down while giving evidence about her lost son, the killer asked the judges if he could smoke a cigar – and was granted permission. And one morning, he protested that there were too many women in court, saying: 'This is a case for men to discuss.'

The names of boys were read to him, and he was asked if he had killed them. 'Yes, that might well be,' he said of 13-year-old Ernest Ehrenberg. 'I'm not sure about that one,' he replied about Paul Bronischewski. And he turned angrily on the anguished father of Hermann Wolf when shown a photograph of the boy.

'I should never have looked twice at such an ugly youngster as, according to his photograph, your son must have been,' he sneered. 'You say your boy had not even a shirt to his name and that his socks were tied on to his feet with string. Deuce take it, you should have been ashamed to let him go about like that. There's plenty of rubbish like him around. Think what you're saying man. Such a fellow would have been far beneath my notice.'

Newspaper reporters in court could not disguise their disgust for the killer, or their sympathy for the relatives of his victims. One journalist wrote:

'Nearly 200 witnesses had to appear in the box, mostly parents of the unfortunate youths. There were scenes of painful intensity as a poor father or mother would recognize some fragment or other of the clothing or belongings of their murdered son. Here it was a hand-kerchief, there a pair of braces, and again a greasy coat, soiled almost beyond recognition, that was shown to the relatives and to Haarmann. And with the quivering nostrils of a hound snuffling his prey, as if he were scenting rather than seeing the things displayed, did he admit at once that he knew them.'

Twice a shudder ran through the court. 'How many victims did you kill altogether?' asked the prosecution. Haarmann replied: 'It might be 30, it might be 40. I really can't remember the exact number.' The prosecution asked: 'How did you kill your victims?' Haarmann replied coldly: 'I bit them through their throats.'

Only when Grans's part in the murders was in doubt did Haarmann lose his composure. 'Grans should tell you how shabbily he has treated me,' he shouted. 'I did the murders, for that work he is too young.' He claimed Grans incited him to kill some victims because he had taken a fancy to the boy's trousers or coat. Grans left him alone overnight to do the murder, returning in the morning for the clothes. Once, though, he was too impatient. Haarmann told the court: 'I had just cut up the body when there was a knock at the door. I shoved the body under the bed and opened the door. It was Grans. His first question was, "Where is the suit." I sat down on the bed and buried my face in my hands . . . Grans tried to console me, and said: "Don't let a little thing like a corpse upset you." '

The cold-hearted cynicism of Grans aroused more horror in court than the unsophisticated blundering of Haarmann. The younger man denied every accusation, but there was never any doubt that both would be convicted. Haarmann knew that, and his main concern throughout was that he was not found insane. Early in the trial he shouted: 'Behead me, don't send me to an asylum.' And after two psychiatrists declared him mentally sound, the court decided he should have his wish.

THE MASS-MURDERER OF HANOVER

Twelve armed policemen faced the public gallery on the day of judgment, 19 December, 1924, after anonymous threats that Haarmann would be shot in revenge for his monstrous crimes. The courtroom was packed as sentence of death was pronounced on him. Grans was jailed for life, later commuted to 12 years.

Haarmann remained to the end. On the last day he screamed:

'Do you think I enjoy killing people? I was ill for eight days after the first time. Condemn me to death. I only ask for justice. I am not mad. It is true I often get into a state when I do not know what I am doing, but that is not madness. Make it short, make it soon. Deliver me from this life, which is a torment. I will not petition for mercy, nor will I appeal. I want to pass just one more merry evening in my cell, with coffee, cheese and cigars, after which I will curse my father, and go to my execution as if it were a wedding.'

Next morning, Haarmann was beheaded, and the town of Hanover was at last free from the curse of the worst mass-murderer in modern history. No-one will ever know exactly how many teenage boys he and Grans massacred – but one police source guessed that, during their final 16 months, they were killing two every week.

The Sadistic Romeo

NEVILLE HEATH

Neville George Clevely Heath had the looks that boys' comic heroes are made of. His wide, blue eyes and fair, wavy hair set off a fresh-complexioned face which had women swooning. And his suave charm around the clubs and restaurants of London ensured that he was never short of a pretty companion when the evening ended. Girls fell for his impeccable manners, and his tales of derring-do in the war that had just finished. But Heath's handsome face hid a terrible secret. Possibly bored with the conventional sex that was so readily available to him, he began pandering to a sadistic streak. And in the summer of 1946, that perversion turned him into a ladykiller in every sense of the word.

Heath was then 29, and well known to both the police and the armed forces. He had served time in civilian jails for theft, fraud and false pretences. He had been court-martialled by the British RAF in 1937 (absent without leave, escaping while under arrest and stealing a car), the British Army in 1941 (issuing dishonoured cheques and going absent without leave) and the South African Air Force in 1945 (undisciplined conduct and wearing unauthorized decorations). In April 1946, he was fined £10 by magistrates at Wimbledon, London, for wearing medals and a uniform to which he was not entitled. By then, unknown to the authorities, he was also indulging in much more sinister fantasies.

A month earlier, the house detective at a hotel in London's Strand burst into a locked room after other guests reported hearing screams. He found Heath standing over a naked girl who was bound hand and foot, and being savagely whipped. Neither she nor the hotel wanted any publicity, and Heath was allowed to slink away. But in May he was at it again. This time he had a more willing victim, a 32-year-old masochist called Margery Gardner. She was a film extra, separated from her husband, and known as Ocelot Margie to doormen at the clubs where she turned up in an ocelot fur coat, looking for men prepared to satisfy her craving for bondage and flagellation. Heath was more than ready to oblige, but when he took her to the Pembridge Court Hotel in Notting Hill Gate the hotel detective again intervened after hearing the sound of flesh being thrashed.

Ocelot Margie did not learn from her escape. When Heath phoned her a few

Margery Gardner with inset of Neville Heath

weeks later, she agreed to meet him on Thursday, 20 June. After drinks at one of Heath's favourite haunts, the Panama Club in South Kensington, they took a taxi back to the Pembridge Court, where Heath had booked in four days earlier with another girl who had since left. It was after midnight when they arrived. Guests in adjoining rooms heard nothing to disturb their slumbers that night.

At 14.00 next day, a chambermaid entered Room 4 on the first floor of the 19-bedroom hotel and recoiled with horror when she drew back the curtains. The two single beds were bloodied and disordered. And in one of them lay the lifeless body of Ocelot Margie. She was naked, her ankles bound tightly together with a handkerchief. Her face and chin were bruised, as if someone had used intense force to hold her mouth closed. There were 17 criss-cross slash marks on her face, front and back. Her breasts had been badly bitten. And she had been bleeding profusely from the vagina.

Police forensic experts quickly built up a grisly picture of the indignities inflicted on the woman before her death from suffocation. Her wrists also showed signs of being tied together, though the bond had been removed and was missing. The killer had washed the face of the corpse, but left dried blood in the nostrils and eyelashes.

On Saturday Heath was in Worthing, Sussex, wining and dining the girl with whom he had first occupied the room in Notting Hill. She was Yvonne Symonds, a 19-year-old who had met the chilling charmer at a dance in Chelsea seven days earlier, and only consented to spend the following night with him after accepting his whirlwind proposal of marriage. Now she was back at her parents' home. Heath booked into the nearby Ocean Hotel, and took her for dinner at a club at Angmering.

There he told her his version of the murder in the room they had shared. He said he met the victim on the evening of 20 June, and she asked to borrow his room to entertain another man, since they had nowhere else to go. Heath claimed he slept elsewhere, and was taken to the room by an Inspector Barratt next day and shown the body. It was, he told Yvonne, 'a very gruesome sight.' He added that the killer must be 'a sexual maniac.'

Both Yvonne and her parents were puzzled next morning to read in the Sunday papers that police were looking for Neville George Clevely Heath. Surely they had already seen him? Yvonne rang Heath at the Ocean Hotel, and he told her he was going back to London to clear up what must be a misunderstanding. He did indeed leave Worthing – but not for London. He went further down the south coast, to Bournemouth, where he booked in at the Tollard Royal Hotel as Group Captain Rupert Brooke.

Before he left Worthing, he posted a letter to Inspector Barratt at Scotland Yard. The two had never met, but Heath, who signed the letter with his real name, said he felt duty bound to report what he knew of the murder in his room.

He again said Margery Gardner asked for his keys, but said she was obliged to sleep with the other man for mainly financial reasons. She hinted that, if Heath arrived back at 02.00 she would spend the rest of the night with him. He arrived at the appointed time, found her 'in the condition of which you are aware', then panicked and fled because of his 'invidious position'.

Heath gave a fictitious description of the other man – a slim, dark-haired character called Jack – and curiously added: 'I have the instrument with which Mrs Gardner was beaten and am forwarding this to you today. You will find my fingerprints on it, but you should also find others as well.'

The instrument never arrived, though Inspector Barratt was not surprised by that. Yet despite his suspicions, increased by the letter, Scotland Yard did not issue a photograph of the wanted man. Heath was thus able to enjoy himself in Bournemouth for 13 days, drinking freely, going to shows, and chatting up holidaymaking girls at dances. On 3 July, he invited the friend of one of his dancing partners to tea, and they got on so well that a dinner date was fixed for that night at his hotel. Just after midnight, Heath left to walk her home along the promenade. He was asleep in his own bed at 04.30 when the night porter checked, not having seen him return.

Two days later, the manager of the nearby Norfolk Hotel reported one of his guests missing. Miss Doreen Marshall, a 21-year-old from Pinner, Middlesex, had last been seen leaving for dinner at the Tollard Royal. The manager there asked 'Group Captain Brooke' about his guest, and suggested he contact the police. Heath duly called at the station, identified the girl from photographs, and consoled her anguished father and sister.

But an alert detective constable thought the handsome six-footer fitted a description Scotland Yard had sent them. Heath was asked if he was the man wanted for questioning about a murder in London. He denied it, but was delayed long enough for other officers to take a good look at him. When he complained of feeling cold as the evening drew in, an inspector went to the Tollard Royal to collect Heath's jacket. And in the pockets was all the evidence the police needed.

As well as a single artificial pearl and the return half of a first class rail ticket from London to Bournemouth, there was a left-luggage ticket issued at Bournemouth West station on 23 June. It was for a suitcase which contained clothes labelled Heath, a bloodstained neckerchief, a scarf with human female hairs stuck to it, and a vicious-looking leather-bound riding crop, with a criss-cross weave. The end had worn away, and there was blood on the exposed wires.

Heath was taken to London and charged with the murder of Margery Gardner. On the same evening, 8 July, the body of his second victim was discovered. A woman walking her dog in a deep, wooded valley called

Branksome Chine, a mile west of the Tollard Royal, noticed swarms of flies around a rhododendron bush. She called the police, having read of the missing girl. And officers found a sickening sight.

Doreen Marshall was naked except for one shoe. Her battered body had been covered with her underwear, her inside-out black dress and yellow jacket. Her ripped stockings, broken pearl necklace and powder compact were discarded close by. Her wrists were tied and the inside of her hands ripped, as if she had been trying to avert the blade of a knife. One of her ribs was broken and sticking into her lung, as if someone had knelt on her. And her flesh had been mutilated – mercifully, as forensic experts later proved, after she had been killed with two deep cuts across the throat.

Heath told police that he left Doreen near Bournemouth pier, and watched her walk towards her hotel through some public gardens. He then returned to his own hotel at around 00.30, and because he knew the night porter would be waiting for him, decided to play a practical joke on him, climbing to his room via a builder's ladder left outside. He described it as 'a small deception'. The police dismissed the whole statement as a great deception. And on Thursday 24 September, Heath was charged at the Old Bailey, London, with the murder of Margery Gardner.

His guilt was easily proved. And because he had subsequently killed again, Heath was unable to use what might have been a plausible defence – that Ocelot Margie willingly submitted to whipping and beating, and died accidentally when things got out of hand. Heath knew the game was up, and wanted to plead guilty and accept his punishment coolly and calmly. But his defence counsel persuaded him, against his better judgement, to plead insanity. The attempts of a psychiatrist called on his behalf to try to prove that insanity provided the only memorable moments of the two-day trial.

Dr William Henry de Bargue Hubert, a former psychotherapist at Wormwood Scrubs jail, and one of the leading practising psychiatrists of the day, was utterly discredited by the prosecution cross-examination. A year later, he committed suicide.

Under close questioning from Mr Anthony Hawke for the prosecution, Dr Hubert claimed Heath knew what he was doing when he tied up and lashed Mrs Gardner, but did not consider or know it to be wrong. Did he then think it was right, Dr Hubert was asked. Yes came the reply. 'Are you saying, with your responsibility, that a person in that frame of mind is free from criminal responsibility if what he does causes grievous bodily harm or death?' asked the astounded Hawke. Hubert said he was, because sexual perverts often showed no regret or remorse.

Hawke then asked: 'Would it be your view that a person who finds it convenient at the moment to forge a cheque in order to free himself from financial responsibility is entitled to say that he thought it was right, and therefore he is free from the responsibility of what he does?' Hubert: 'He may think so, yes.'

Hawke: 'With great respect, I did not ask you what he thought. I asked whether you thought he was entitled to claim exemption from responsibility on the grounds of insanity.' Hubert: 'Yes, I do.'

Hawke: 'You are saying that a person who does a thing he wants to do, because it suits him at the moment to do it, is entitled, if that thing is a crime, to claim that he is insane and therefore free from responsibility?' Hubert: 'If the crime and the circumstances are so abnormal to the ordinary person, I do.'

It was an extraordinary thing to claim, and even Heath knew the doctor was harming, not helping, his case. He passed anguished notes to his own counsel, urging him to drop the insanity ploy.

In 1946 the dividing line between the noose and being confined in a mental hospital was the difference between psychopath and psychotic. Psychopaths were considered able to control their evil urges, psychotics were not. In Heath's case, two Home Office prison doctors said he was certainly abnormal, a sadistic sex pervert, but as a psychopath, he was not insane.

The jury of 11 men and one woman found him guilty after only an hour's consideration, and Heath was sentenced to death. He did not bother to appeal, expressed no remorse or sympathy for the families of his victims, and refused to discuss his life or beliefs with any of the experts sent to examine him. He spent most of his last days writing letters, one of which was to his parents: 'My only regret at leaving the world is that I have been damned unworthy of you both.'

He was hanged at Pentonville Prison in London on 26 October, 1946.

The Heartless Husband

JOHANN HOCH

Johann Otto Hoch had never believed in very long courtships or in long marriages. He had at least 24 wives in 15 years – and he brutally murdered all of them. The diabolical 'Bluebeard' even proposed to his sister-in-law over the deathbed of his wife, who was dying from a massive dose of arsenic. She accepted. 'Life is for the living.' Hoch told her. 'The dead are for the dead.'

Throughout Hoch's bizarre years of marriage and murder in the United States between 1892 and 1905, a tough Chicago cop named George Shippy stalked him relentlessly. Shippy knew Hoch was cutting a bloody trail of murder but was never able to prove it.

Born Johann Schmidt in 1862, Hoch had emigrated from Germany at 25 leaving his wife and three children behind. A big, jovial man with a sweeping handlebar moustache, he found work in the country as an itinerant bartender.

From 1887 to 1895 it was anybody's guess how many women he murdered. In April 1895 he found a woman in a saloon in Wheeling, West Virginia. Using the name Jacob Huff, he married her and then killed her three months later.

As with his other murders, the doctor thought the woman died of kidney disease for which there was no cure. But the lady's pastor knew better and Hoch fled from the town after converting his wife's estate to cash. Leaving his clothes and a suicide note behind, he walked naked into the River Ohio. A hundred yards up he had anchored a boat with new clothing in it. He clambered aboard and rowed to the Ohio side.

In 1898, using the name Martin Dotz, the murderer ran foul of Inspector George Shippy. The killer was arrested in Chicago on a minor swindling charge. But the Wheeling preacher saw a newspaper photo, recognized Jacob Huff and contacted Shippy.

Hoch breezed through a year in the Cook County jail while Shippy backtracked the man's elusive trail and investigated dozens of unsolved cases of murdered women. The determined cop went to Wheeling and had the body of Hoch's ex-wife exhumed, only to find that Hoch had removed many of the woman's vital organs.

After serving his sentence, Hoch married and murdered another 15 women between 1900 and 1905. His weapon was always arsenic, which was easily available in any drugstore. The victims were always lonely but wealthy women overwhelmed by Hoch's animal charm. And slipshod doctors were always too quick with the wrong diagnoses.

By now Hoch was acting like a man possessed. He slipped like a ghost from city to city, murdering in record time. Frequently he married and murdered in less than a week.

In 1904 he buried his last victim, Marie Walcker, and promptly married her sister. He fled with his new wife's savings account and the enraged woman contacted Shippy. Her sister's body was exhumed and this time the medical examiner found enough arsenic to kill a dozen women.

Shippy then made his long-awaited arrest.

Throughout the trial Hoch maintained an air of boyish innocence. Even after the guilty verdict, Hoch was confident he would never swing from the gallows.

As guards led him to the scaffold on 23 February, 1906, the killer joked and said: 'You see, boys, I don't look like a monster, now do I?' Nobody answered the question as Hoch's massive hulk fell through the trapdoor.

East End Terror

JACK THE RIPPER

On 25 September, 1888, a letter was delivered to the Central News Agency in London's Fleet Street. It read:

'Dear Boss, I keep on hearing that the police have caught me. But they won't fix me yet . . . I am down on certain types of women and I won't stop ripping them until I do get buckled.

Grand job, that last job was. I gave the lady no time to squeal. I love my work and want to start again. You will soon hear from me, with my funny little game.

I saved some of the proper red stuff in a ginger beer bottle after my last job to write with, but it went thick like glue and I can't use it. Red ink is fit enought, I hope. Ha, ha!

Next time I shall clip the ears off and send them to the police just for jolly.'

The letter was signed 'Jack the Ripper'. It was the first time the name had ever been used. And it immortalized this twisted and mysterious killer who lurked in London's backstreets.

Jack the Ripper's reign of terror was a short one. He first struck on a warm night in August 1888. On a chill, foggy night three months later he claimed his last victim. He is known to have slaughtered at least five women – and some criminologists have credited him with 11 murders.

All that is known for certain about Jack the Ripper is that he had some medical knowledge and that he was left-handed – a fact obvious to police surgeons who examined the grisly remains of his victims. He was probably a tall, slim, pale man with a black moustache. This was the description given by witnesses, including one policeman who saw someone hurrying away from the vicinity of one of the crimes. Each time, he wore a cap and a long coat, and he walked with the vigorous stride of a young man.

But it is unlikely that anyone will ever be able to identify him. Even in 1992, when the secret Scotland Yard files on the case are finally made public, they are expected to cast little new light on the case.

The story of London's most mysterious and ferocious mass-murderer began shortly after 05.00 on the morning of 7 August, 1888. A man hurried down the stairs of the Whitechapel hovel in which he had a room – to be confronted by a

From the Evening News

bundle lying on the first floor landing. He tried to push the bundle out of his way, then recoiled with horror when he realized that what lay at his feet were the bloody remains of a woman. She was identified as Martha Turner, a prostitute. Her throat had been slit, she had been stabbed several times, and bestial mutilations had been carried out on her body.

As the murder of prostitutes was no rare thing in those days, the case was soon shelved. But when a second, similar murder was committed 24 days later, fear and panic began to sweep the mean streets of the East End. The mutilated body of 42-year-old Mary Ann Nicholls – or Pretty Polly as she was known – was found in the early hours of 31 August.

Mary had probably taken no heed of the grisly fate of Martha Turner. She was desperate for money. She needed fourpence for a doss-house bed, and when a tall, pale man approached her she looked forward to the chance of making a few coppers, with perhaps something left over for a couple of tots of gin.

The man drew her into the shadows. If she finally realized there was anything wrong, it was too late. The Ripper put a hand over her mouth and dexterously slit her throat. Then the crazed killer set about his savage butchery. A detective who examined the body said: 'Only a madman could have done this.' And a police surgeon said: 'I have never seen so horrible a case. She was ripped about in a manner that only a person skilled in the use of a knife could have achieved.'

93

Two extracts from *The Illustrated Police New*

THE WORLD'S MOST INFAMOUS MURDERS

It was just one week before the Ripper struck again. His prey was 'Dark Annie' Chapman, 47 years old and dying of tuberculosis when she was hacked down. When found in Hanbury Street by a porter from nearby Spitalfields Market, her few pitiful possessions had been neatly laid out beside her disembowelled corpse.

The next victim was Elizabeth 'Long Liz' Stride. On the evening of Sunday, 30 September, a police constable spotted a white-stockinged leg sticking out from a factory gate. Unlike earlier cases, Elizabeth Stride's body had not been mutilated – which led police to surmise that the Ripper had been disturbed in his grisly task. But, to satisfy his bloodlust, he soon found another victim. And it was during this killing that he left the only clue to his identity.

Just 15 minutes walk from the spot where Long Liz's body had been found was discovered the bloody remains of 40-year-old Catherine Eddowes. Her body was the most terribly mutilated so far – the Ripper had even cut off her ears. And from the corpse a trail of blood led to a message scrawled in chalk on a wall: 'The Jewes are not men to be blamed for nothing.' But this vital piece of evidence was never studied properly. Sir Charles Warren, head of the Metropolitan Police, perhaps fearing a violent backlash of hatred aimed at the Jews, ordered the slogan to be rubbed out and kept a secret.

Rumours now began to sweep like wildfire through the sleazy streets of London's East End. . . . . . The Ripper carried his instruments of death in a little black bag – and terror-crazed crowds chased any innocent passer-by carrying such a bag. He was a foreign seaman – and anyone with a foreign accent went in fear of opening his mouth for fear of being set upon. He was a Jewish butcher – and latent anti-Semitism already simmering because of the influx of Jewish immigrants fleeing the Russian and Polish pogroms began bubbling to the surface.

An even wilder theory, popular in the most squalid areas where there was no love lost between the inhabitants and the police, was that the killer was a policeman. How else would he be able to prowl the streets at night without creating suspicion?

The killer was in turn thought to be a mad doctor, a homicidal Russian sent by the Czar's secret police trying to cause unrest in London, a puritan obsessed with cleansing the East End of vice, and a crazed midwife with a hatred of prostitutes.

On 9 November, the Ripper struck again. Mary Kelly was unlike any of the other victims. She was younger – only 25 – blonde and she was attractive. The last person to see her alive was George Hutchinson whom she had asked for money to pay her rent. When he said he could not help she approached a slim, well-dressed man with a trim moustache and a deerstalker hat. She was never seen alive again.

EAST END TERROR

Early next morning, Henry Bowers knocked impatiently at her door for his unpaid rent. Finally he went to the window of Mary's room and pushed aside the sacking curtain. The sickening sight within made him forget all about the rent and sent him running for the police. Later, he was to say: 'I shall be haunted by this for the rest of my life.'

With Mary Kelly's death, the Ripper's reign ended as suddenly and mysteriously as it began.

Two convicted murderers claimed to be the Ripper. One, who poisoned his mistress, said when arrested: 'You've got Jack the Ripper at last.' But there is little evidence to suggest that he was telling the truth. The second cried out as the trapdoor on the gallows opened 'I am Jack the . . .' But it was later proved that he was in America when the Ripper crimes were committed.

Some members of the police force were sure they knew who the Ripper was. In 1908, the assistant commissioner of police said flatly: 'In stating that he was a Polish Jew, I am merely stating a definitely established fact.'

But Inspector Robert Sagar, who played a leading part in the Ripper investigations and who died in 1924, said in his memoirs:

'We had good reason to suspect a man who lived in Butcher's Row, Aldgate. We watched him carefully. There was no doubt that this man was insane, and, after a time, his friends thought it advisable to have him removed to a private asylum. After he was removed, there were no more Ripper atrocities.'

Even Queen Victoria's eldest grandson has been named as a suspect. He was Prince Albert Victor, Duke of Clarence, who, if he had lived, would have become king when his father, Edward VII, died.

But perhaps the most likely solution is the one arrived at by author and broadcaster Daniel Farson. He pointed the finger of suspicion at Montagu John Druitt, a failed barrister who had both medical connections and a history of mental instability in his family.

Farson based his accusation on the notes of Sir Melville Macnaghten, who joined Scotland Yard in 1889 and became head of the Criminal Investigation Department in 1903. Macnaghten named three Ripper suspects – a Polish tradesman, who hated women and was probably Jewish, a homicidal Russian doctor, and Druitt.

The soundest basis for blaming Druitt for the murders is that a few weeks after the death of Mary Kelly, Druitt's body was found floating in the River Thames. After that, there were no further attacks by Jack the Ripper

The One Who Got Away

BELA KISS

I f the term 'kiss of death' had not already existed, headline writers would have invented it to describe Bela Kiss. For the well-to-do, middle-aged Hungarian murdered at least 23 people before 'dying' on a battlefield during World War One, and escaping to freedom in America. He is one of the few mass murderers to evade justice.

Kiss was 40 when he arrived in the Hungarian village of Czinkota in 1913 with his beautiful, 25 year-old bride Maria. He had bought a large house and taken on servants, and the locals soon warmed to the man who collected stamps, grew roses, and did a little writing, especially on astrology. From time to time he would drive to Budapest on business in his smart red car, and the village policeman, Adolph Trauber, readily agreed to keep an eye on the home of the man with whom he had struck up a close friendship.

War was clearly only months away, and Constable Trauber was not surprised when his friend started returning from Budapest with oil drums. Kiss explained they were full of petrol so that he could continue his business trips when fuel became scarce. Trauber decided to keep quiet about the fact that, while Kiss was away, his wife was entertaining a young artist called Paul Bihari. But the affair was common knowledge among villagers and servants at the house. And they sympathized when, after another trip to Budapest the distraught husband emerged from his empty home to show them a note, saying the couple had eloped together.

For several months, Kiss shut himself away, refusing to see anyone, even Trauber. But in the spring of 1914, the constable persuaded him to rejoin the world, and found him an elderly widow to act as housekeeper. Kiss resumed his journeys to the Hungarian capital, returning each time with more oil drums. He told Trauber that the petrol was in payment of a debt owed to him by a Budapest garage owner. But Kiss brought other things from Budapest – women, not young like Maria, but sometimes even older than himself. Several times his housekeeper stormed out when her kitchen was invaded, only to return when Kiss told her the offending female had left.

Kiss and Constable Trauber spent many evenings together in conversation, and during one of their chats, the policeman mentioned the disappearance of two widows in Budapest. They had vanished after answering a lonely hearts advertisement in a newspaper, placed by a man named Hofmann. Both had drawn heavily on their savings after meeting him. Kiss joked that he too had had some unsuccessful affairs with middle-aged widows, and both men laughed.

War broke out that August, but Kiss was not among the first to be called up. He continued his trips to Budapest, returning with more oil drums and more women. When he was eventually conscripted, he left the house and his petrol stockpile in Trauber's care. And the constable continued to look after them after May 1916, when news arrived that Bela Kiss had been killed in action.

Later that summer, soldiers arrived in Czinkota looking for petrol. Trauber remembered the oil drums, and led the way to where they were stood. But a horrific discovery awaited him. Instead of petrol, each of the seven drums in the house contained alcohol. And each contained the doubled-up body of a naked woman.

Detectives called in from Budapest combed the gardens, and dug up yet more drums, each containing a grisly secret. In all, there were 23 tin-can coffins. The victims, who included faithless Maria and her lover, had all been garotted. Letters found in the house made it clear that Kiss and lonely-heart Hofmann were the same person, and that he had taken money or possessions from each of his fatal conquests. But there was nothing police could do: Their quarry had died at the front. The file was closed.

Then, in 1919, a friend of one of the victims recognized Bela Kiss crossing Margaret Bridge in Budapest, and reported the sighting to police. Shocked detectives discovered that Kiss had exchanged identities with a fallen colleague during the war, but before they could find him, he vanished again.

In 1924, a deserter from the French Foreign Legion told French police of a colleague called Hofmann, who had boasted of garotting exploits. But by then Hofmann, too, had deserted. It was ten years before he was again recognized, in Times Square, New York. And in 1936, he was reportedly working as a janitor at a Sixth Avenue apartment block. Fellow Hungarians there described him as a small, plain, inoffensive man in his middle sixties, a man with a bleak future. Bela Kiss did not talk about his even bleaker past.

The Vampire of Düsseldorf

PETER KURTEN

He is the king of sexual delinquents . . . he unites nearly all perversions in one person . . . he killed men, women, children and animals, killed anything he found.' Those were the chilling words used to describe Peter Kurten, the Vampire of Düsseldorf, at his trial in 1930. They came not from the judge, nor the prosecution, but from defending counsel, pleading for a verdict of insanity. But Kurten, 47, did not escape the execution his reign of terror so richly deserved, because the court agreed with the verdict of one of the top psychiatrists called to examine the callous killer: brutal sadist Kurten 'was at the same time a clever man and quite a nice one.'

Psychopaths ran in the Kurten family, and young Peter, the fifth child in a family of 13, saw the exploits of one at first hand in his home at Cologne-Mulheim. His father would arrive home drunk, beat the children, and sexually violate his unwilling wife in front of them. He also committed incest with his 13-year-old daughter, and Kurten followed his father's example with her. From the age of nine, he also had another teacher. The local dog catcher initiated him to torturing animals. Kurten was an enthusiastic pupil, and progressed from dogs to sheep, pigs, goats, geese and swans. What excited and aroused him most was the sight of their blood. He frequently cut the heads off swans and drank the blood that spurted out.

Soon Kurten switched his attentions to human victims. As a boy he had drowned two playmates while all three swam around a raft in the Rhine. By the age of 16, he was living with a masochistic woman who enjoyed being beaten and half-strangled. She had a daughter of 16, and all three enjoyed a sordid co-existence, interrupted only when Kurten's attempts at theft and fraud landed him in prison. He was later to claim that the inhumanity and injustice of his treatment in jail led to his blood-soaked career as a killer. In fact prison provided him with another outlet for sadism. He deliberately broke prison rules to gain solitary confinement, where he indulged his erotic reveries.

'I thought of myself causing accidents affecting thousands of people,' he was to recall in court. 'I invented a number of crazy fantasies such as smashing bridges and boring through bridge piers. Then I spun a number of fantasies with regard to bacilli which I might be able to introduce into drinking water and so cause a great calamity. I imagined myself using schools and orphanages for the purpose, where I could carry out murders by giving away chocolate samples containing arsenic. I derived the sort of pleasure from these visions that other people would get from thinking about a naked woman.'

When he was freed from prison, Kurten began to turn his daydreams into nightmare reality. He became an arsonist – 'the sight of the flames delighted me, but above all it was the excitement of the attempts to extinguish the fire and the agitation of those who saw their property being destroyed.' And he began to attack defenceless women and children.

His first attempt at murder was unsuccessful. He admitted leaving a girl for dead after assaulting her during intercourse in Düsseldorf's Grafenburg Woods. But no body was ever found. It was assumed that the girl recovered enough to crawl away, to ashamed or scared to report the incident. Eight-year-old Christine Klein was not so lucky. She was found in bed, raped and with her throat cut. Her uncle was arrested and tried, and though aquitted for lack of evidence, the shame of the charge stuck to him until he died during World War One. Kurten must have enjoyed that. His own trial was shocked by the detailed, fussy, matter-of-fact way he related what had really happened, 17 years earlier.

'It was on 25 May, 1913,' he recalled in the clipped, precise tone that only made his deeds seem more ghastly. 'I had been stealing, specializing in public bars or inns where the owners lived on the floor above. In a room above an inn at Cologne-Mulheim, I discovered a child asleep. Her head was facing the window. I seized it with my left hand and strangled her for about a minute and a half. The child woke up and struggled but lost consciousness.

'I had a small but sharp pocketknife with me and I held the child's head and cut her throat. I heard the blood spurt and drip on the mat beside the bed. . . The whole thing lasted about three minutes, then I locked the door again and went home to Düsseldorf. Next day I went back to Mulheim. There is a cafe opposite the Klein's place and I sat there and drank a glass of beer, and read all about the murder in the papers. People were talking about it all around me. All this amount of horror and indignation did me good.'

Kurten was not prepared to use his sadism on the Kaiser's behalf when war broke out. He deserted a day after call-up, and spent the rest of the hostilities in jail, for that and other minor crimes. Released in 1921, he decided to marry, and chose a prostitute at Altenburg as his bride, overcoming her reluctance by threatening to kill her. He gave up petty crime and went to work in a factory as a moulder. He became an active trade unionist, and a respected pillar of society, quiet, charming, carefully dressed and meticulous about his appearance – even a little vain. Those who knew he was having affairs with other women did not tell his wife. And the women were not prepared to confide that Kurten was a rough lover, who enjoyed beating and half-choking them.

But once Kurten and his wife moved to Düsseldorf in 1925, blood lust again got the better of him. Though his relations with Frau Kurten remained normal, his assaults on his mistresses became more vicious. Soon he was attacking innocent strangers with scissors or knives, aroused by the sight of their blood. As he escaped detection, he stepped up the rate of attacks, varying his style to cover his tracks. By the summer of 1929, the town of Düsseldorf was in the grip of terror. Police had pinned 46 perverted crimes, including four killings, down to someone who seemed to have vampire tendencies. But they had not clues as to the monster's identity.

On the evening of 23 August, two sisters left the throng at the annual fair in the suburb of Flehe to walk home through nearby allotments. Louise Lenzen, 14, and five-year-old Gertrude stopped when a gentle voice sounded behind them. 'Oh dear, I've forgotten to buy cigarettes,' the man said to Louise. 'Look, would you be very kind and go to one of the booths and get some for me? I'll look after the little girl.' Louise took his money and ran back to the fair. Kurten quietly picked up her sister, carried her into the darkness behind a stand of beanpoles, and efficiently slaughtered her, strangling her and cutting her throat with a Bavarian clasp knife. When Louise returned, he pocketed the cigarettes, accepted his change – and did the same to her.

Twelve hours later, a servant girl called Gertrude Schulte was stopped by a man who offered to take her to a fair at nearby Neuss. As they strolled through woods, he attempted to rape her, but she fought him off. He produced a knife, and began stabbing her in a frenzy, piercing her neck, shoulder and back. When he threw her to the ground, the knife snapped, leaving the blade in her back.

Gertrude was lucky – her screams alerted a passer-by, and she was rushed to hospital. But Kurten had escaped again. The newspapers continued to report his exploits with mounting hysteria. In one half hour, the 'Vampire' attacked and wounded a girl of 18, a man of 30 and a woman of 37. Later he bludgeoned serving girls Ida Reuter and Elizabeth Dorrier to death. And on 27 November he slashed five-year-old Gertrude Albermann with a thin blade, inflicting 36 wounds on her tiny body.

Gertrude was the last victim to die, but the attempted murders and vicious attacks continued through the winter and early spring, attracting headlines across Germany. Maria Budlick, a 21-year-old maid, had read the stories while working in Cologne, 30 kilometres away, but when she lost her job, she boarded a train for Düsseldorf, her desperation for employment outweighing any fears about the vampire.

It was 14 May, 1930, when she stepped on to the platform at Düsseldorf, and

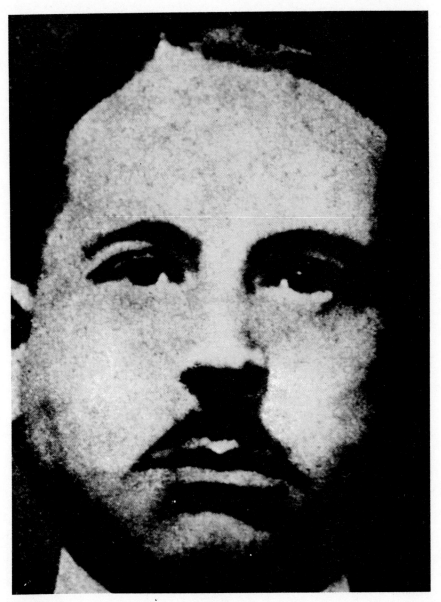

Peter Kurten

was soon approached by a man who offered to show her the way to a girls' hostel. She accompanied him happily through the streets, but when he turned into the trees of Volksgarten Park, she drew back. The man assured her she had nothing to fear, but she refused to be placated. As they argued, another man emerged from the shadows and asked: 'Is everything all right?' Maria's escort left, and she was left alone with her rescuer – Peter Kurten.

Convinced that he had saved her from a fate worse than death, or death itself, Maria agreed to go with him to his home for a meal. Kurten gave her a glass of milk and a ham sandwich, then offered to take her to the hostel. They boarded a tram – but for the second time in less than an hour, poor Maria was being misled. Her rescuer led her straight into Grafenburg Woods, on the northern edge of town, then lunged at her, gripping her throat and attempting to rape her against a tree. Maria struggled, but the man was too strong for her. Then, as she was about to pass out, he let go of her, and asked: 'Do you remember where I live, in case you ever need my help again?'' Maria gasped: 'No.' Kurten escorted her out of the woods, and left her.

Maria had remembered where he lived, but surprisingly she did not go to the police. Instead, she wrote about her ordeal to a friend in Cologne. The letter was incorrectly addressed, and opened at the post office to be returned to the sender. An alert official realized the implications of its contents and contacted the authorities. Next day, plain clothes detectives took Maria back to the street she remembered, Mettmannerstrásse, and she identified Number 71 as the home of her assailant. She also saw Kurten, but he vanished before she could tip off her police escort.

Kurten had also seen Maria, and realized that the net was closing in on him. He went to the restaurant where his wife worked, and confessed everything to her. He had never felt guilt for his crimes, and even admitting them now did not affect his appetite. He ate not only his own meal, but the one his shocked wife could not touch. On the morning of 24 May, Frau Kurten went to the police, and told them she had arranged to meet her husband outside a certain church at 15.00. Armed officers surrounded the area, and when Kurten arrived four rushed at him, revolvers pointing at his chest. He smiled and offered no resistance, saying: 'There is no need to be afraid.'

In his 15-year career of law-breaking, Jesse James murdered about 10 people and stole about $200,000. He was also one of Quantrill's Raiders who massacred 150 inhabitants of Lawrence, Kansas. He was shot in the back by his cousin, Bob Ford, while fixing a picture on his cabin wall in St Joseph, Missouri, in 1882.

THE VAMPIRE OF DÜSSELDORF

> Hungarian countess Elizabeth Bathory bathed in the blood of her victims because she believed it preserved her beauty. In the black depths of her castle dungeons at Csejthe, the countess stored well-fed girls ready to have their veins cut open and filtered into pipes that ran into a blood bath. When her blood craving reached a peak, she would nibble one of her victims to a premature death.
>
> Tried for 610 murders, the countess was sentenced to be walled up for life in a room from which all light and sound were excluded. In 1614, she expired after three years of this living death.

The trial, when it opened in a converted drill-hall at Düsseldorf's police headquarters on 13 April, 1931, was almost a foregone conclusion. Thousands surrounded the building to try to catch a glimpse of the man who had admitted 68 crimes, apart from those for which he had already served time, while being questioned. He was charged with nine murders and seven attempted murders, and the prosecution hardly needed to produce any evidence to gain a conviction – Kurten admitted everything coldly, calmly, and in astonishing detail. Sleek and immaculate, he confessed to being a sex maniac, a rapist, a vampire, a sadist, an arsonist. He gave chapter and verse about his bestiality, his jail fantasies, and how he had strangled, stabbed and clubbed women and children to death. He admitted drinking blood from one woman's cut throat, from a wound on a man's forehead, from the hand of another victim. he described how he had enjoyed reading about Jack the Ripper, and how he had visited a waxworks Chamber of Horrors, and promised himself: 'I'll be here one day.'

A shoulder-high cage had been built round the accused man's stand to prevent him escaping. Behind him were the exhibits – the knives and scissors he had used to kill, the matches he had used to burn property, the spade he had used to bury one woman, the skulls of the innocent strangers he had butchered for the sake of an orgasm. The judge treated him gently, guiding him carefully through the catalogue of appalling crimes. There was no need to be tough, Kurten was as mild-mannered and courteous as his unsuspecting neighbours had always known him. But by the time it came to the prisoner's final speech, even the hardened judge was sickened.

Incredibly, Kurten, who had blamed his childhood and prison for turning him into a killer, now began preaching puritanically about the behaviour of others. He said:

> 'My actions as I see them today are so terrible and horrible that I do not even make an attempt to excuse them. But one bitter thing remains in my mind. When I think of the two Socialist doctors accused recently of

abortions performed on working class mothers who sought their advice, when I think of the 500 murders they have committed, then I cannot help feeling bitter.

The real reason for my conviction is that there comes a time in the life of every criminal when he can go no further, and this spiritual collapse is what I experienced. But I do feel that I must make one statement: some of my victims made things very easy for me. Man-hunting on the part of women today has taken on such forms that . . .'

The judge could stand no more unctuous rhetoric, and angrily banged his desk for silence.

The jury took 90 minutes to find Kurten guilty on all accounts, and he was sentenced to death nine times. On 1 July, 1932, he chose veal, fried potatoes and white wine for the traditional last meal, and enjoyed it so much that he asked for second helpings. At 06.00 next morning he marched to the guillotine in Cologne's Koingelputz prison, and was beheaded after declining the attorney general's offer of a last wish.

But the twisted mind of Kurten had had one final wish. He asked the prison psychiatrist, minutes before he left his cell for that last walk, 'After my head has been chopped off, will I still be able to hear, at least for a moment, the sound of my own blood gushing from the stump of my neck?' As the appalled official sat stunned in silence, Kurten smiled and said: 'That would be the pleasure to end all pleasures.'

The Killer Who Kept Quiet

HENRI DESIRE LANDRU

F ew murder trials in history have aroused so much controversy, as that of
Henri Desire Landru at Paris in November 1921. He was accused of 11
murders, but the prosecution could produce no bodies, no proof of how
he killed his victims, and no proof of how he disposed of them. The jury
convicted him on circumstantial evidence, then petitioned for mercy. Eventually Landru went to the guillotine still protesting his innocence – and even
today, there are those who believe him.

The court proceedings themselves degenerated into farce. France was
demob-happy after World War One, and hungry for entertainment. The
French government was happy to divert attention from the peace talks at
Versailles which were going badly. A nation that still holds romancers in high
esteem could not resist the small, thin, bald, strange-looking man with deep-set,
flickering black eyes who was said to have made the acquaintance of 283 ladies
in five years. In court, men roared and cheered as this curious Casanova baffled
his frustrated accusers by resolutely refusing to discuss his amours. Women blew
him kisses and made blatant gestures of sexual invitation. When one woman
arrived late in the packed courtroom, Landru earned applause by gallantly
getting to his feet, and offering her his seat in the dock.

The facts of the case, alas, were less romantic. Henri Desire Landru was a
small-time thief and swindler well-known to the police since his first arrest in
1900. He had progressed from petty pilfering to conning widows and lonely
spinsters out of their savings via lonely-heart matrimonial advertisements in the
Paris newspapers. But he was not very good at it. As soon as his dupes realized
he was only interested in their money, many went to the police. Landru was in
and out of prison until 1914. His father, a respectable ironworker who had
retired to the Dordogne, committed suicide in 1912 when he came to visit his
son, only to find him in jail for fraud.

By July 1914, the French judicial system had had enough of Landru. He was
convicted, in his absence, of a motor cycling business swindle, and sentenced to
four years, with a recommendation that he be banished to the penal
establishment in New Caledonia as a habitual criminal. Landru, who had a
wife and four children, was on the run, knowing that one mistake would mean
transportation and exile. Yet he needed money to live. His answer, according to

the prosecution at his trial, was chillingly simple. He continued to seduce willing ladies for profit, but ensured that they would not complain to the authorities by murdering them.

Had the French police not been undermanned and fully stretched because of the war, Landru could never have survived for so long. He had a distinctive, disproportionately big red beard, which later earned him the inevitable nickname 'Bluebeard', and he continued to visit his old haunts around Paris, particularly the garages where he hoarded stolen goods. It was at one of them, in February 1914, that he had met Madame Jeanne Cuchet.

She was 39, a widow working in a Paris store, and was accompanying her son Andre, 18, who had applied to Landru for a job. She quickly became infatuated with the smooth-talking man who called himself M. Diard, said he was a well-to-do engineer, and wore an impressive violet ribbon, an 'Order' he had invented and bestowed upon himself. Madame Cuchet's married sister was suspicious of Diard, however, and went so far as to break into his villa at Chantilly, discovering letters from several women addressed to a variety of differently-named men. But Madame Cuchet was not to be deterred.

She agreed to her lover's suggestion of renting a villa called The Lodge at Vernouillet, on the outskirts of Paris, and happily paid six months rent. They moved in on 8 December, 1914, and the woman and her son were last seen alive in the garden the following 4 January. By that time Madame Cuchet's family had washed their hands of her, and though she was later reported missing, the inquiries into her whereabouts were almost non-existent.

Encouraged by this success, which netted him about 15,000 francs in jewels, furniture and securities, Landru embarked on another conquest. Madame Therese Laborde-Line was 47, a widow with little money and no relatives in France – she came from Buenos Aires, Argentina. Recklessly using the name Cuchet, Landru wooed her and won what she possessed. He took her to Vernouillet in June 1915, and she too vanished there.

This was convenient for Landru, for on 11 May, he had placed this advertisement in the Paris morning paper, *Le Journal*: 'Widower with two children, aged 43, with comfortable income, affectionate, serious and moving in good society, desires to meet widow with a view to matrimony.' Three of the women who answered the advertisement that May were to disappear before the year was out.

Madame Désiree Guillin was 51, a former governess with a legacy of 22,000 francs. She was delighted at the prospect of going to Australia as the wife of 'diplomat M. Petit', and happily went to The Lodge with him on 4 August. She was never seen again. Landru sold her furniture and forged her signature to get at her bank balance. The bank should have spotted that, but again the war was the excuse.

THE KILLER WHO KEPT QUIET

Henri Desire Landru

THE WORLD'S MOST INFAMOUS MURDERS

Landru decided to leave The Lodge for somewhere more secluded. He picked the Villa Ermitage, a large, sparsely-furnished house in a little-used side road near the village of Gambais in the department of the Seine. It was close to the forest of Rambouillet just outside Paris, with several lakes and ponds nearby. One of the few improvements Landru made was to install a small stove. Then he was ready to entertain guests.

The first was Madame Heon, a 55-year-old widow who replied to the May advertisement, and fell for 'M. Petit', now head traveller for a large South American company. She was last seen alive at Gambais in December, which left Landru free to pursue his wooing of the third likely candidate from his advertisement, Madame Anna Collomb.

She was 44 – though she discreetly put her age at 29 in her letter to him – and a widow. Landru had at first told her he was M. Cuchet, a war refugee from Rocroi who had a factory at Montmartre, and she fell for him, she told her mother, 'because he is a real gentleman and says such beautiful things to me.' The infatuated woman moved in with him at a flat in the Rue Chateaudun, and gave him her furniture to put in store. When she visited Gambais with him, she found he was known there as M. Fremyet. Landru explained to her suspicious mother that he used two names to secure a double war indemnity, a fact that confirmed her opinion of him as a crook. But Anna's love was unshakeable. On Christmas Eve, she invited her sister Madame Pelat to Gambais, and Landru spoke warmly of his plans to marry Anna and move tò Nice. Madame Collomb was not seen again after 27 December.

Landru was 8,000 francs richer when he met his next lover, a 19-year-old serving girl, on the Paris Métro in January. Though she was penniless, Andree Babelay was pretty, and he dallied with her for nearly four months. She was last seen on 12 April at Gambais, after which Landru renewed his acquaintance with 44-year-old Madame Celestine Buisson, another widow who agreed to trust him with her furniture and securities. She disappeared on 17 August.

Three more ladies were to take a one-way trip to Gambais: Madame Louise Jaume, 38, a devout Catholic separated from her husband, who vanished only hours after she and Landru knelt in prayer at a church in November, 1917; Madame Anne-Marie Pascal, 33, a divorcée, who seemingly bequeathed Landru her false teeth and umbrella when she disappeared in April, 1918 – he sold them for 30 francs – and Madame Marie-Therese Marchadier, 37, a lodging house keeper with a lurid past who was seen no more after 13 January, 1919. Landru then cleared everything from her Paris apartment.

But by then the web of deceit Landru had woven was slowly being unravelled. Madame Pelat, sister of Anna Collomb, was puzzled when she received no replies to letters she sent to the Villa Ermitage. She wrote to the mayor of Gambais, asking if he knew the whereabouts of M. Cuchet-Fremyet.

THE KILLER WHO KEPT QUIET

Shortly before, the mayor had had another letter, from Mademoiselle Lacoste, the sister of Madame Buisson, inquiring about the man she had called on at the villa, M. Dupont. The mayor wrote to both women, suggesting that they contact each other. When they met, it did not take long to discover that Cuchet-Fremyet and Dupont were one and the same man.

The two women went to the police, and the name Cuchet rang a bell. Madame Cuchet and her son were still listed as missing after going away with a man named Diard. The coincidence seemed too strong to be ignored. And the description of the wanted man – small, bald, with a big red beard – also fitted an engineer named Guillet, suspected of fraud and theft. On 10 April, 1919, an arrest warrant was issued.

Just one day later, the search was over. Mlle Lacoste was walking in the Rue de Rivoli when she spotted the man she knew as Dupont strolling arm-in-arm with a smartly-dressed young woman. She followed them into a shop, and heard them order a white china dinner service. Mlle Lacoste lost the couple in the crowds, but went straight to the police, who discovered that the china had been ordered in the name of Lucien Guillet. Early next morning, they swooped on the address he had given, No 76 Rue de Rochechouart.

Landru at first protested that he was Guillet, born at Rocroi in 1874. But when he was searched, he tried to throw a small, loose-leaved black book out of the window. That book was to send him to the guillotine. For Landru had been insanely meticulous about keeping details of his affairs. He had listed each reply to his lonely hearts advertisements under seven headings – to be answered *poste restante*; without money; without furniture; no reply; to be answered to initials *poste restante*; possible fortune; to be investigated. He had noted every expense, even down to the two sous he put in the collection box when he went to church with Madame Jaume. More seriously, he had described the tickets bought for his trips to Gambais – a return one for himself, a single ticket for his ladies.

On the front cover of the book he had written in pencil: Cuchet, J. *idem*, Bresil, Crozatier, Havre, Buisson, A. Collomb, Babelay, Jaume, Pascal, Marchadier. The police knew only three names on the list at that stage, but they were enough for them to arrest Landru for murder. Painstaking investigations revealed that women answering to the names Babelay, Jaume, Pascal and Marchadier had also vanished, that Bresil denoted Madame Laborde-Line (Landru may have muddled Argentina and Brazil), that Madame Guillin lived in the Rue Crozatier, and that Madame Heon came from Havre.

Police searched the Villa Ermitage on 9 April but found nothing. After the arrest, they raided all Landru's properties, and discovered intimate papers and identity cards for all the missing women, plus clothes and personal trinkets belonging to them. They also found two wax cords, of the type sometimes used to strangle people. On 29 April, they returned for a thorough search of the villa at Gambais. Sifting through ashes beside the stove, they came across 295 fragments of bone, as well as fastenings from parts of buttons and other remains of women's clothing.

The French judicial system involves a preliminary interrogation by an examining magistrate, with wide-ranging powers to prepare the ground for a trial. An able inquisitor called Bonin was assigned to Landru. Aided by witnesses and the best advice from crime experts, he questioned the little man for two-and-a-half years, going over and over the evidence in the black book, warning him that forensic experts had identified the bone fragments as being from three human bodies, asking him about each missing woman in turn. Landru took refuge in his right, under the law, to remain silent.

To most questions, he replied: 'I have nothing to say.' Occasionally he would tell Bonin: 'I am a gallant man. I cannot allow you to ask me questions concerning the ladies. If they have disappeared, it is nothing to do with me. I know nothing of what became of them. Discover proofs, bring them to me, and then I will discuss them with you.' Another time, Bonin said: 'You are a murderer.' Landru replied: 'You say so. Prove it. Look, investigate, imagine, but prove it if you can.'

Asked about Madame Cuchet, he said: 'Her hiding place is a secret between herself and me. I am a man of honour, and though I understand the accusation you have brought, I will not reveal it. I have given my word.' When Bonin pointed out that she had broken off contact with her closest friends, Landru replied stonily: 'Madame Cuchet was heartbroken by the hypocrisy of the world, as I am.'

It was a remarkable feat of endurance by Landru, particularly as he was weakened by attacks of gastritis. The authorities had evidence that black, acrid smoke had been seen coming from the chimney at Gambais, and that a man answering Landru's description had been seen throwing a package into a lake near the Villa Ermitage. The bones of Madame Marchadier's two griffon dogs had been dug up in the grounds. But there was still no concrete proof of murder, and no bodies. Nonetheless, in France, unlike Britain, a man was guilty until proved innocent.

In September 1921, M. Bonin sent the result of his examinations – 7,000 documents – to the Department of Criminal Prosecution. The trial began at the Versailles Palais de Justice on 7 November. Landru was only 52, but his illness and prison pallor made him look like a weary old man. It took three hours for the clerk to read the indictment – an astonishing catalogue of seduction, swindling, forgery and multiple murder. Landru seemed indifferent, reacting only when the phrase 'exploitation of women' was read out.

On the second day of the trial, the court president questioned the prisoner, who disputed some facts in his statement, saying: 'The police are often inefficient.' When asked why he had not co-operated with M. Bonin, Landru said: 'It is not my business to guide the police. Have they not been accusing me for the past three years of deeds which the women who disappeared never for one moment reproached me with?' The president stifled a burst of laughter in court with the words: 'It is you who have made it impossible for these women to complain.'

Landru claimed the names in his book were all business clients. He bought their furniture, ready to sell it back to them once the Germans had left France. When the prosecution pointed out that, on one day, he had met six or seven women, Landru replied: 'That proves well that I was not concerned with any affairs.' He claimed the matrimonial advertisements were an innocent business ruse, 'to flatter their conceit'. But again he refused to discuss details of his dealings with the women, saying they were 'private matters'.

Landru parried some questions with black humour. Asked what had become of Madam Guillin, he said: 'It is not for me to say, it is for the police to find out. They took six years to find me. Perhaps they will end up finding Madame Guillin.' To the prosecutor, he said: 'I fully recognize, sir, that you are after my head. I regret that I have not more than one head to offer you.'

But on one occasion, a witness wiped the smile from his face. Madame Friedmann, sister of Jeanne Cuchet, shouted at Landru: 'My sister loved you so much that she would not have left you to be condemned if she had been living.' Then, in hushed tones, she told of a dream in which her sister had appeared before her, and told her that Landru had slit her throat while she slept. Madame Friedmann's sobbing, and the emotional response of the public galleries, forced the session to be adjourned. No court of law could accept dreams as proof of murder. Yet no jury could forget such a powerful moment.

Though no-one had proved that Landru burned any bodies, lengthy testimony from a medical jurist on the effects of burning human remains was allowed. It made grisly listening. 'A right foot disappears in 50 minutes,' the jury was told, 'half a skull with the brains taken out in 36 minutes, a whole skull in 1 hour and ten minutes.'

Civil lawyers representing relatives of the missing women were also allowed to make dramatic accusations against the prisoner, denouncing him as a murderer who chopped up bodies, without a shred of conclusive factual justification.

Faced with a mounting tide of circumstantial evidence against his client, defence attorney Moro-Giafferi one of the most distinguished lawyers in France, put up a brave fight. He produced the girl Landru was with when he was arrested, Fernande Segret, who made the most of her big moment in a sealskin coat and picture hat. She described herself as a 'lyric artist', and no singer could expect a more enthusiastic welcome than she got from the men in the court. When order was restored, she declared that Landru was a good lover, strongly passionate, and that he made her very happy. She said she had cooked for him on the stove at Gambais, where Landru was alleged to have burned the bodies, and had cleared the cinders afterwards without noticing any skulls or bones.

Moro-Giafferi then made an emotionally brilliant speech, saying that under civil law, none of the missing women would have been presumed dead for several years. Why assume they were now, when a man's life depended on it. He claimed that Landru was a white slave trader, who had dispatched the women to brothels in Brazil, and that that was the real reason for the word Brazil appearing in the little black book. But the jury were not prepared to believe that Brazilians had a penchant for middle-aged widows.

There was uproar in court when Landru was convicted. Photographic flashlights exploded, men cheered, women fainted. Moro-Giafferi was shattered. He was convinced his man was not guilty, and immediately drew up a petition for mercy, which the jury signed. Landru, under the sentence of death, found himself in the bizarre position of consoling his crestfallen counsel.

Moro-Giafferi was there on the morning of 25 February, 1922, when Landru went to the guillotine. The prisoner refused offers of Mass and confession, and waved aside a tot of rum and a cigarette. Asked if he had anything to say, he retorted: 'Sir, to ask such a question at such a time is an insult. I have nothing to say.' But he turned to Moro-Giafferi, shook his hand, and said: '*Maître*, I thank you. You have had a desperate and difficult task to conduct. It is not the first time that an innocent man has been condemned.'

Landru begged them not to cut off the bushy red beard of which he was so proud. They merely trimmed it. Followed by his lawyer and the rejected priest, he walked out into the cold dawn air, shivering slightly with the cold, and muttering: 'I will be brave.'

His death solved none of the still unanswered questions. Had he killed all the women? If so, how? And how had he disposed so expertly of them, the murder weapons, and any other tell-tale clues? If he killed for money, why did he kill a penniless serving girl and the impecunious Madame Pascal? Was it because they discovered papers relating to the other women? Those questions will probably never be answered, despite an alleged confession printed by newspapers in 1968. The reports claimed that a framed picture given to a defence lawyer had the words, 'I did it, I burned their bodies in my kitchen oven' scribbled on the back.

The intriguing Landru story has two other odd postscripts. On the night before his execution, he wrote a letter to the man who had prosecuted him, the Advocate General *Maître* Godefroy, which was said to have greatly distressed the man. It read:

THE KILLER WHO KEPT QUIET

'Why could you not meet my gaze when I was brought back to court to hear my sentence? Why did you so indignantly rebuke the crowd for its unseemly behaviour? Why today are you still seeking for the vanished women, if you are so certain that I killed them?

It was all over. Sentence had been pronounced. I was calm. You were upset. Is there a conscience that troubles uncertain judges as it ought to trouble criminals? Farewell, *Monsieur*. Our common history will doubtless die tommorow. I die with an innocent and quiet mind. I hope respectfully that you may do the same.

Nearly 50 years after the execution, a film called *Landru*, scripted by novelist Françoise Sagan, was released. To the film-makers' astonishment, Landru's last mistress, Fernande Segret, turned up and sued them for 200,000 francs damages. She got 10,000. Since nothing had been heard of her for years, she had been presumed dead. In fact, she had been working as a governess in the Lebanon. After winning her case, she retired to an old people's home in Normandy. But the money did not buy her peace. She drowned herself, because she was tired of being pointed out as 'the woman in the Landru case.'

The Monster of the Andes

PEDRO LOPEZ

The guards fingered their pistols and watched nervously as the steel door to cell 14 was unlocked. There, in Ambato Jail, high up in the Andes mountains in Ecuador, was the man who held the world's most horrible distinction.

Inside, cowering in a corner of his cell in the women's section of the prison, was Pedro Alonzo Lopez. He was petrified that he might be burned alive, or castrated, by the other inmates or the guards themselves. Lopez, known in South America as 'the Monster of the Andes' had admitted to murdering 300 young girls. Lopez has been credited with being the world's worst mass sex killer, with the highest ever tally of victims.

Like most mass killers, Lopez' motive was sex. Before the 300 were strangled, they were first raped. Lopez did away with girls in this fashion at the rate of two a week for the three years he was on the rampage.

In Ambato alone, nestling 3,000 metres up in the Andes, the killer took police to the secret graves of the bodies of the 53 girls all aged between 8 and 12. At 28 other sites he described to police, bodies could not be found because the graves had been robbed by prowling animals. Some of the girls' bodies were buried at construction sites, and police have had to assume that they are now encased in concrete, perhaps never to resurface. Others are under roads.

In his confessions, Lopez admitted to killing 110 girls in Ecuador, another 100 in neighbouring Colombia and 'many more than 100' in Peru. Retired Major of Police, Victor Hugo Lascano, director of Ambato prison, said: 'We may never know exactly how many young girls Lopez killed. I believe his estimate of 300 is very low, because in the beginning he co-operated and took us each day to three or four hidden corpses. But then he tired, changed his mind and stopped helping.'

Lopez was eventually charged with 53 of the murders but another charge listed 110 more bodies named in his confession. Major Lascano said: 'If someone confesses to 53 you find, and hundreds more that you don't, you tend to believe what he says. What can he possibly invent that will save him from the law?'

In his cell in the women's section of Ambato Prison, Lopez was kept out of immediate danger from enraged guards and male prisoners. The women prisoners were considered to be in no danger themselves 'because his sex drive was geared only to young children.'

This mass child-killer was born the seventh son in a family of 13 children. His mother was a prostitute in the small Colombian town of Tolima, who threw him out onto the streets when he was eight for sexually fondling one of his younger sisters. A stranger found the boy crying and hungry, took him in his arms and promised to be his new father and care for him. Instead, the stranger took young Pedro to a deserted building and raped him. For the rest of his life, Lopez would be afraid to sleep indoors.

'I slept on the stairs of market places and plazas', he told police. 'I would look up and if I could see a star, I knew I was under the protection of God.'

In Bogota, an American family fed and clothed the street urchin, and enrolled him in a Colombian day school for orphans. When he was 12 he stole money from the school and ran away with a middle-aged woman teacher who wanted to have sex with him.

At 18 he stole a car and drove across Colombia. He was caught and jailed. On his second day in prison he was raped in his cell by four male prisoners. Lopez made himself a crude knife. Within two weeks, according to the story he told police, he had murdered three of the men: the fourth stumbled across their bodies and ran screaming through the prison. Lopez was given an additional two-year sentence for the killings, which were deemed self-defence.

Released from jail, Lopez found himself excited by pornographic magazines and movies. But he was afraid of women and therefore unable to communicate with them. 'I lost my innocence at the age of eight', he told police, 'so I decided to do the same to as many young girls as I could.'

By 1978, Lopez had killed more than 100 Peruvian girls, many of them belonging to indian tribes.

His crimes first came to light when he was caught by Ayacucho indians in the northern sector of Peru as he carried off a nine-year-old girl. They stripped and tortured him, then put him in a deep hole . . . they were going to bury him alive.

An American woman missionary saved his life. She convinced the indians that they should not commit murder. She took Lopez in her jeep to the police outpost. Within days he had been deported; the police did not want to bother with dead indian girls at that time. Only later, when the full story emerged, was a proper investigation begun.

Across the border in Ecuador the real killing spree then began. 'I liked the girls in Ecuador' Lopez told police. 'They are more gentle and trusting, and more innocent. They are not as suspicious of strangers as Colombian girls.'

Lopez would walk through market squares seeking out his victims. He said he deliberately sought out young girls with 'a certain look of innocence'. In graphic detail he told police how he would first introduce the children to sex, then strangle them.

I would become very excited watching them die.' 'I would stare into their eyes until I saw the light in them go out. The girls never really struggled – they didn't have time. I would bury a girl, then go out immediately and look for another one. I never killed any of them at night, because I wanted to watch them die by daylight.'

Police in the three countries were by now collating information, but they still did not realize they were looking for a mass killer. Their main theory was that an organization had been kidnapping the girls and transporting them to work as maids and prostitutes in large cities.

In April 1980, a rain-swollen river overflowed its banks near Ambato and horrified townspeople discovered the remains of four missing girls. Police launched a manhunt, but it was unsuccessful.

Days later, Carlina Ramon Poveda, working in the Plaza Rosa market, discovered her 12-year-old daughter Maria was missing. Frantically, she ran through the plaza, calling for her. She saw her walking out of the market, holding a stranger's hand.

Carlina followed her daughter and the tall man to the edge of town and then called for help. A dozen local indians jumped on Lopez and pulled him to the ground. They held him until the police arrived.

In jail awaiting trial, Lopez was tricked by police into making a confession. A priest, Pastor Cordoba Gudino, masqueraded as a fellow prisoner. For a month he stayed locked in the same cell as Lopez, and developed a behind-bars friendship with him. From the information he gave Gudino, the Ecuadoran police were able to extract a full confession from Lopez. Subsequent liaison with the police forces of Colombia and Peru substantiated Lopez's story.

Convicted of the murders in Ecuador, Lopez received a life sentence, which, in that country, means a maximum of 16 years, with good behaviour he could be a free man by 1990. Had he been convicted in Colombia, Lopez would be dead. There, the penalty for murder is death by firing squad.

The Murderous 'Family'

CHARLES MANSON

C harles Manson preached bloody revolution and ruled a satanic cult who killed at his bidding. He was sentenced to die in the gas chamber, but with the death sentence now abolished in California he is serving nine life sentences for nine murders. On his orders, his followers slaughtered the actress Sharon Tate, the wife of film producer Roman Polanski, and three friends at her Hollywood home in August, 1969.

Two nights later he sent his followers into action again to butcher close neighbours of the Polanskis, supermarket owner Leno la Bianca and his wife Rosemary. He was also found guilty of beheading stuntman Donald Shea and of ordering the execution of musician Gary Hinman.

Manson, 48, is the illegitimate son of a prostitute. When he was young his mother and brother were jailed for beating and robbing men she picked up.

At 11, Manson fell foul of the law and was sent to reform school. He spent the next 21 years in penal institutions, emerging at 32 never having slept with a woman or drunk a glass of beer. Confused by freedom, he caught a long-distance bus chosen at random and alighted at San Francisco's Haight-Ashbury district, centre of the world hippie movement.

It was 1967, the height of the peace-and-love flower-power era. Manson grew his hair long, wore a beard and played the guitar. Soon he had a circle of admirers. Girls came to kneel at his feet. One said: 'The first time I heard him sing, it was like an angel. He was magnetic.' Another, Lynette 'Squeaky' Fromme, said: 'With Charlie, I was riding on the wind. Making love with Charlie was guiltless, like a baby.'

But Manson had little respect for women. At the commune he set up in the Hollywood hills, they outnumbered men four-to-one. One of the rules of his 'family' was that the dogs had to be fed before the women. Girls had to submit instantly to the men Manson named. He banned contraceptives, alcohol and the wearing of spectacles. Questions by the girls were forbidden and they could not use the word 'Why?' But they worshipped him as a god.

Women would travel miles to ask him to sleep with them. A film actress who begged for his favours was told to first climb a nearby mountain. Another woman brought along her 15-year-old daughter. Manson told the mother to go because she was too old, and to leave her daughter. She obeyed.

THE WORLD'S MOST INFAMOUS MURDERS

Charles Manson, in the chapel of Vacaville jail, California

THE MURDEROUS 'FAMILY'

Manson's incredible magnetism gave him an entry to the wilder fringe of the Hollywood party circuit. It is almost certain he and some of his followers had been entertained by the Polanskis before the night Sharon and her friends died.

The slaughter was the culmination of months of testing to which Manson had subjected his disciples. Bored with their simple adoration of him, he started to organize law-breaking exercises. He made them steal cars, commit petty thefts and prowl round people's homes in 'creepy-crawling' black clothes. Then he ordered them to Sharon Tate's house to terrorize a man whom he said had broken several promises to him.

Polanski was in Europe making a film, and he asked an old friend, Voytek Frykowski and his girlfriend Abigail Folger, to move in with Sharon to keep her company.

On the evening of 8 August, Jay Sebring, Sharon's ex-lover and now a friend, had dropped in too. They and an 18-year-old youth visiting Frykowski, were to die horribly that night at the hands of three girls and an ex-football star, trusted members of Manson's inner circle. Sharon, who was eight months pregnant, was stabbed 16 times. The word 'Pig' was written in her blood on the front door.

Today the man whose reign of bloody terror stunned the world is serving out his sentence as caretaker of the prison chapel at Vacaville, in southern California. He is unrepentant about the past, claiming to feel no guilt for the bestial crimes committed at his command. He told the British photographer Albert Foster: 'I am not ashamed or sorry. If it takes fear and violence to open the eyes of the dollar-conscious society, the name Charles Manson can be that fear.'

Inset: Sharon Tate with Roman Polanski at their wedding, 1968

Bad But Not Mad

PETER MANUEL

Sentencing Peter Thomas Anthony Manuel to death at Glasgow in May, 1958, the judge Lord Cameron said: 'A man may be very bad without being mad.' Manual, who callously killed at least nine people, certainly qualified as very bad. But does a sane man pick victims at random, murder for no apparent reason, attempt to extort money from a man he has made a widower, then eagerly offer the evidence that will lead him to the gallows?

Manuel was certainly no fool. Halfway through his trial, he dismissed his lawyers and conducted his own defence so well that Lord Cameron congratulated him on his peformance. He used legal knowledge studied during his frequent prison sentences for burglary, theft, indecent assault, rape and violence. But he forgot one vital fact: in Scotland, a multi-murderer is charged with every killing. In England, on the other hand, he would have been charged with only one of them, on the grounds that evidence of other crimes might prejudice a jury unfairly.

Manuel's astonishing record as a killer reads like that of a gangster in Chicago, and he would have been proud of the comparison. He was, in fact, born in America. His parents left Scotland for New York in the 1920s, and Peter was born there in 1927. But the Depression forced them back to Britain, and their misfit son was soon in trouble. By the time he was 16, a senior probation officer said he had the worst record he had ever known in a boy. In January 1956, Manuel added murder to that record.

Anne Kneilands was just 17 years old. She was waiting for her boyfriend in an East Kilbride street when Manuel met her. He had rugged, Teddy Boy good looks, and she agreed to go to a nearby cafe with him. But as he walked her home later, he suddenly dragged her into a wood, and smashed her to death, beating her skull with a piece of iron.

Police were baffled by the seemingly motiveless attack. They interviewed all the possible suspects on their books, including Manuel, but put the scratches on his face down to Hogmanay excesses. Manuel had had enough police interviews in his life to know exactly what to say.

During that summer Manuel, the rebel without a cause, decided he needed a gun. His criminal ego was growing. He had killed once and got away with it. He could do it again.

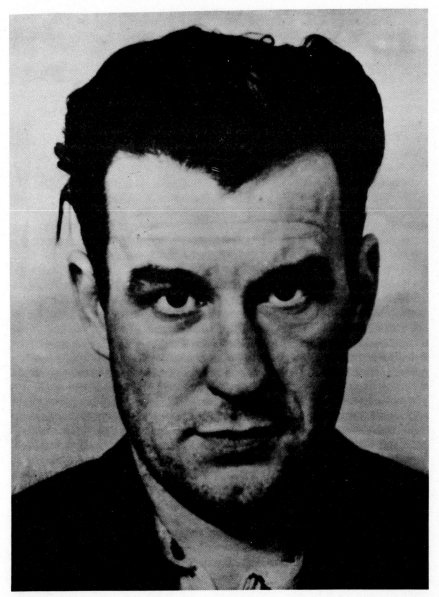

Peter Manuel

Isabelle Cooke, murdered in January, 1958

On 16 September, 1956, he and two other men and a woman went on a robbery expedition to the wealthy area of High Burnside, a few miles south of Glasgow. They plundered one empty house, and even started a drinking party there. Manuel pointed out another home nearby, but the others were reluctant to stage a second break-in. Manuel went alone.

Getting in on the ground floor, he went straight upstairs, and saw two women asleep in one room. He opened another bedroom door, and saw 16-year-old Vivienne Watt. She was awake, and sat up in fear when she spotted him. Manuel bounded across the room, knocked her out and tied her up. Then he returned to the other room. Mrs Marion Watt, a semi-invalid and Vivienne's mother, was still asleep. So was her sister, Mrs Margaret Brown. Manuel calmly drew his gun and shot them both at close range. Then he walked back to Vivienne, who had come round and was struggling with her bonds. Holding her roughly down on the bed, he shot her through the left eye.

Manuel interfered with the night-dresses of all three women but, again, did not touch them. Expert witnesses later declared that he got sexual satisfaction from killing without the need for contact. It was 03.00 when he rejoined his pals in the first house, and about 05.00 when they went back to Glasgow.

But Manuel's shot had not killed Vivienne instantly. Her body was still warm when the family's daily help arrived next morning. And if that gave Manuel added satisfaction, the next development delighted his twisted mind. Police arrested Mrs Watt's husband, William, and accused him of the three murders.

Mr Watt, a baker, had been staying at a hotel in Lochgilphead, Argyll, 80 miles away, on the night of the killings. Witnesses had seen him there at midnight and 08.00. But police proved it was possible for him to have driven to his home and back comfortably in those eight hours. And they had witnesses who swore they had seen Mr Watt in his car on the Renfrew Ferry at 03.00.

The unfortunate man spent two months in prison before he was set free. The police could find no reason why a prosperous, loving father would kill his happy family. But Mr Watt's ordeal was not over. For Peter Manuel, who had equally little reason for killing his loved ones, now tried to extort money from the bereaved man. First he told Watt's solicitor he could name the Burnside murderer for a price. Then he met Mr Watt, and offered to remove lingering suspicions by killing the Burnside murderer, and making it look like suicide. It would only cost £120. The baker declined.

Manuel was playing with fire, but amazingly he got away with it. And he was also continuing to kill. On 8 December, 1957, he took a train to Newcastle upon Tyne, south of the border. He then took a taxi and ordered Sidney Dunn, the driver, to a deserted moorland road near Edmondbyers, then shot and stabbed him. Just after Christmas, he met 17-year-old Isabelle Cooke on the outskirts of Glasgow, dragged her into a field, tore off most of her clothes, and strangled her.

He then buried the girl he had never seen before in a shallow grave.

While the rest of Scotland was sleeping off Hogmanay, Manuel broke into the Glasgow bungalow of Peter Smart on New Year's Day, 1958. He found £25 in a wallet, and could have left undetected because Mr Smart, his wife Doris and their son Michael had not heard a thing. Instead, Manuel went into their bedrooms and shot all three dead. Then he calmly fed two tins of salmon to the family cat.

But at last Manuel had made a mistake. Under routine surveillance as he was after every major crime, he was seen passing some new blue £5 notes – notes of the type Peter Smart had drawn from the bank before his death. The home Manuel shared with his parents was searched, and after discovering house-breaking equipment, the police arrested both Manuel and his father. Manuel then agreed to make a statement on condition his father was released.

What he told them was an emotionless, detailed story of his murders. The cold-blooded confession stunned hardened officers, who reported that, when he led them to Isabelle Cooke's grave, he said almost light-heartedly: 'This is the place. In fact, I think I'm standing on her now.'

Manuel craved the limelight, and longed to be feared as a big man. But neither the police, nor the court, were awed by his exploits. After listening to 250 witnesses and a three-hour closing speech from Manuel himself, the jury found him guilty of seven of the eight murders with which he was charged – the Newcastle killing was outside Scottish jurisdiction, and the killing of Anne Kneilands was not proven for lack of evidence.

Peter Manuel, a particularly vicious and wanton murderer, was hanged at Glasgow's Barlinnie Prison on 11 July, 1958.

The Prince of Poisoners
WILLIAM PALMER

Williamilliam Palmer has gone down in history as the Prince of Poisoners, a murderer so notorious that the town where he practised his evil arts applied to the prime minister for permission to change its name. Palmer's trial has been hailed as the most sensational of the nineteenth century. What made it so was not that he was the first prisoner to use strychnine, but the incredible story of debauchery and lust that unfolded. For Palmer and his wretched relatives were leftovers from an earlier age. And an England trying to get used to the puritanism of Queen Victoria lapped up each lurid detail of Palmer's Regency lifestyle – sex, gambling, drinking, scandal. . . and murder.

Palmer was born in Rugeley, Staffordshire, in 1824, the second son of a sawyer who had swindled his employer, the Marquess of Anglesey, out of £70,000 by selling his timber, and a woman whose uncle had fathered an incestuous granddaughter by his own illegitimate daughter. Such a heritage need not have brough out the worst in young William – four of his brothers and sisters led perfectly normal lives. But his eldest sister, Mary Ann, turned to promiscuity, taking after her mother; his brother Walter became an alcoholic; and William himself turned to a life of wine, women and gambling – funded by theft and fraud.

His father died when he was 12, but any hopes William had of enjoying a life of leisure on his legacy were dashed when he received only a £7,000 share of the ill-gotten fortune. When Palmer left school, he was apprenticed to a Liverpool firm of chemists, Evans and Evans, but the demands of his heavy flutters on the horses, entertaining the ladies, and keeping up with the rich, idle circle of friends he formed soon exhausted his allowance. Palmer began stealing money sent with orders he collected for the firm from the Post Office. He was soon discovered and sacked.

His mother settled the bill for the missing cash and sent him to work for a surgeon, Edward Tylecote. Though outwardly industrious and ambitious, Palmer was more intent on profit and profligacy than medicine. He stole from his employer and took advantage of his position to seduce his patients. It is estimated that he fathered 14 illegitimate children during the five years he worked for Tylecote. Eventually the surgeon lost patience with his troublesome assistant, and enrolled him as a 'walking pupil' at Stafford Infirmary. Palmer quickly found that this in no way lessened his opportunities for sex and stealing, and he also grabbed the chance to indulge a new passion – poisons. The hospital authorities were so alarmed by his activities that they barred him from the dispensary, but Palmer was not so easily rebuffed.

In 1846, an inquest was held at Stafford into the death of a man called Abley. He had been unwise enough to accept a challenge to a drinking bout from Palmer, who was having an affair with his wife. After only two tumblers of brandy, Abley was violently sick, and died within minutes. Though the authorities were suspicious, nothing could be proved against Palmer, who left shortly after the death to continue his studies at St Bartholomew's Hospital in London. In retrospect, most experts believe Abley was the poisoner's first victim in what may have been a toxicological experiment.

Palmer squandered more than £2,000 during a riotous year in London – an enormous sum in those days – and only just managed to qualify as a doctor. But in one subject he was top of his class. The only note he made in one of his textbooks was: 'Strychnine kills by causing tetanic fixing of the respiratory muscles.'

In August 1846, Palmer was back in Rugeley, setting up his practice in a large house opposite the Talbot Arms Inn. The lascivious reputation of both his widowed mother and himself made the locals far from eager to put their lives in his hands, and Palmer had few patients to keep him away from his first love, the race track. But already he was tumbling into debt, and was anxious to cut his expenditure in other directions. One day he asked to see the illegitimate daughter he had fathered by a maid he had known when working for Dr Tylecote. She died shortly after returning to her mother the same evening. Soon other illegitimate offspring unaccountably suffered fatal convulsions after licking the honey their fond father spread on his finger.

In 1847, Palmer took himself a wife. Ann Brookes was herself illegitimate. Her father, an Indian Army colonel, had committed suicide, and her mother, the colonel's former housekeeper, had taken refuge in drink. Both were well provided for, the widow inheriting property worth £12,000, the daughter living on the interest of £8,000 capital as a ward of court. One of her two guardians was a cousin of Palmer's former employer, Dr Tylecote, and was opposed to the marriage, but Palmer successfully asked the courts for permission to wed their charge. From all accounts, the two were very much in love, and their happiness was clouded only by the way their children kept dying. Four were killed by mysterious convulsions when only days or weeks old between 1851 and 1854. Only the eldest boy, Willy, survived.

Several of Palmer's relatives and racing companions were not so lucky. He called on his uncle, Joseph Bentley, a drunken degenerate, and suggested a trial

THE PRINCE OF POISONERS

A note written by William Palmer to his council while in the dock at the Old Bailey

of drinking strength. Again, sharing brandy with Palmer proved a sickening experience. The uncle died three days later, leaving his nephew a few hundred pounds. In 1848, Palmer invited his mother-in-law to stay at Rugeley. Though an alcoholic, she still had enough of her wits about her to detest her daughter's husband. She confided to a friend before the journey to Rugeley: 'I know I shan't live a fortnight.' She died ten days after arriving.

That nobody found anything suspicious in the deaths of those around Palmer was due in large measures to his performance as an actor. To the community, he was a respected, church-going, unctious man, charming, pious, kind and generous. His wife believed he was doing his best to save her mother when he gave her medication and personally prepared her food.

Palmer also allayed suspicion by calling in a second opinion, a good-hearted, doddering local doctor named Bamford, who was over 80 and prepared to agree with his young friend's diagnoses. When Palmer told him death was due to apoplexy or English cholera, Bamford obligingly signed death certificates to that effect.

The death of Palmer's mother-in-law was not as profitable as he expected. Her property was tied up, and what little money accrued to the grieving newly-weds was only a drop in the ocean of the doctor's gambling debts. Already he owed thousands of pounds to a dubious Mayfair lawyer, Thomas Pratt, and lesser sums to Midlands' moneylenders called Padwick and Wright. His attempts to remove his own relatives continued, but when the wife of another uncle became ill while paying him a visit, she refused to take the pills he proferred, throwing them out of a window instead. Palmer managed to explain away the fact that chickens who pecked at the pills were dead next morning.

He turned his attentions to his racing companions. He owed a man called Leonard Bladen £800 after a run of back luck. He invited him to Rugeley, and after a convivial evening, the guest took to his bed with a stomach upset. Within a week he was dead. Bladen's wife, who heard about the illness from a third party, arrived just before the end, but was upset at not being allowed to see the body. She was also perturbed to be told that her husband had only £15 on him, and that Palmer expected £59 from the man's estate to settle a gambling debt. Her friends urged her to go to the police, but she refused, out of consideration for Mrs Palmer. Another gambler called Bly also learned how lethal it could be to win money from Palmer. Mrs Palmer was becoming upset at the string of deaths in the house. 'My mother died here last year, now these men,' she wailed. 'What will people say?'

Towards the end of 1853, Palmer's finances were in a more hopeless state than ever. He backed one of his own horses, Nettle, to win £10,000 in the Oaks. It lost. Twice he was declared a defaulter on bets, and barred from Tattersalls, the Mecca of the racing establishment. Pratt, Padwick and Wright were all becoming increasingly strident in their demands for payment – and interest on his gambling debts was now running into thousands of pounds. Palmer needed money desperately – desperately enough to kill the wife he loved.

In January 1854, the month he poisoned his fourth child, he took out three life insurance policies on Mrs Palmer, for a total of £13,000. They were arranged with the help of Pratt and a local attorney, Jeremiah Smith. Smith was having an affair with Palmer's mother, now aged over 60, but was not anxious for the news to be broadcast. Palmer knew of the liaison, and had used it to pressure Smith into helping him forge his mother's signature on guarantees for his own debts. Now Smith helped to fix up the three life policies – two, with Norwich Union and Sun Insurance, for £5,000 each, one, with the Prince of Wales company, for £3,000. The premium was a total of £760 a year, and apparently none of the companies bothered to ask how a country doctor with little income and a penchant for betting could afford to pay so much. In fact, Palmer borrowed the money from Pratt.

> The Roman Emperor Tiberius was incredibly strong – he could poke his finger through an apple – but his weaknesses were even more dramatic. His lusts knew no bounds. He once broke the legs of two priests when they did not react favourably to his advances. And he would often have his lovers tortured and murdered when he no longer found them amusing.

Palmer managed to tide himself over during the summer, but a fresh cash crisis hit him in September. As luck would have it, his wife returned from visiting relatives in Liverpool with a chill. She took to her bed, and Palmer's devoted care soon turned a minor ailment into chronic antimony poisoning.

This time, he took the precaution of calling in not only Dr Bamford, but also his wife's former guardian, the once-suspicious Dr Knight. He too was now an octogenarian, and, like Bamford, was prepared to concur with Palmer's diagnosis. All three signed a death certificate citing English cholera. Palmer seemed distraught at the death, weeping and sobbing inconsolably. But he still managed to spend that night with his maid, Eliza Tharm, who gave birth to a child exactly nine months later.

At first the insurance companies were reluctant to settle the policies Palmer had taken out such a short time before. They were suspicious at such a sudden death in a seemingly healthy woman of 27. But faced with the verdicts of two doctors of good repute, they decided not to call for an inquest, and Palmer was given his money. He immediately gave £8,000 to Pratt and £5,000 to Wright. But Padwick stepped up his demands, and Pratt was soon insisting on further efforts to settle Palmer's account. Shrugging off the suspicions of the insurance companies, Palmer decided they were the best policy for saving him from ruin.

With Pratt's help, he devised a scheme to cover the life of his brother Walter, a bankrupt dipsomaniac, for an astonishing £82,000. The total was split between six companies, and Palmer persuaded Walter to co-operate by promising to lend him £400, and by offering to provide him with the drinks that Walter's wife was rationing.

The insurance companies, once bitten, were shy about dealing with the Palmer family again. Walter's doctor, a man called Waddell, signed one application form, declaring that his patient was 'healthy, robust and temperate'. But he added in a covering note: 'Most confidential. His life has been rejected in two offices. I am told he drinks. His brother insured his late wife's life for many thousands, and after the first payment she died. Be cautious.'

Palmer finally secured policies to a total of £13,000, invited his brother to Rugeley, and for five months plied him with gin. It has been estimated that Walter drank 19 gallons of the spirit before leaving for home in July, 1855. Palmer arranged to meet his brother at Wolverhampton races on 14 August, and prepared for the encounter by buying some prussic acid. Again Walter embarked on a gin binge, but this time the drinks were laced. Two days later he was dead of an apoplectic fit. By the time his widow learned of his demise, the body was already in its coffin.

Palmer instantly applied for the life insurance policies to be paid up, but the companies delayed settlement until they had investigated further. Palmer would have been wise to wait, but Pratt, who had been assigned the policy on

Walter as security for loans of £11,500, would not let him. In September, he demanded a £6,000 payment. Palmer desperately tried to take out new insurance policies on George Bate, whom he described as a 'gentleman farmer'. When the companies investigated, they found they were being asked to take a £25,000 risk on a penniless undergroom at Palmer's stables.

Palmer was told there would be no policy on Bate's life – and no payment on the insurance for Walter. If he went to court to claim his £13,000, they said, they would counter claim with a charge of murder. Palmer was now in desperate straits. Pratt was threatening to sue for his money by issuing writs against Palmer's mother, the unwitting guarantor. Palmer knew that the penalty for forging signatures was transportation. He also had a new problem to contend with. Some years earlier he had arranged an abortion for a Stafford girl, Jane Burgess, whom he had made pregnant. He unwisely sent her passionate love letters, described by one author who read them as 'too coarse to print'. Palmer had urged the girl to burn them, but she was not that foolish. Now she wrote to him, threatening blackmail.

On 13 November, 1855, Palmer went to Shrewsbury races with his pal John Parsons Cook, a 27-year-old rake who had squandered a £12,000 legacy from his father, but aimed to recoup some of it on his horse Polestar in the Shrewsbury Handicap. To the delight of both men, Polestar won. Cook collected £800 in cash from bets on the course, and unwisely showed Palmer a betting slip from Tattersalls for a further £1,200.

Cook, like Palmer, was generous in sharing his successes. He and a party of friends celebrated the victory with a slap-up champagne supper at the Raven Hotel in Shrewsbury. But after accepting a glass of brandy from Palmer, he was violently ill. He handed over his cash winnings to another man, saying: 'I believe that damned Palmer has dosed me.' Yet he agreed to Palmer's suggestion next morning that he come back to Rugeley for medical treatment.

Cook took rooms in the Talbot Arms, where Palmer, living just across the road, could keep a careful eye on him. On Friday, 16 November, Cook dined with Palmer and Jeremiah Smith. Next morning, he was again violently sick. Palmer kept popping in with medicines, and on the Sunday sent some broth across to the inn. A chambermaid who tasted it while heating it retched for the next five hours, but nobody blamed the broth, and Palmer was allowed to take a bowl up to his friend. Dr Bamford had already been called in for consultations, and by the Monday Cook was feeling a little better. This could have been because Palmer had gone up to London to cash Cook's betting slip at Tattersalls, and pay £450 of it to Pratt.

There could now be no turning back for Palmer. He returned to Rugeley at 22.00, and bought three grains of strychnine from the local surgeon's assistant on his way to the Talbot Arms. That night, Cook went through agony.

Above: The trial of
William Palmer 1856

Right: extract
from Palmer's
diary

Chambermaid Elizabeth Mills was with him. She said later: 'He was sitting up beating the bedclothes with his hands. His body, his hands and his neck were moving then – a sort of jumping or jerking. Sometimes he would throw himself back on the pillow and then raise himself up again. He screamed three or four times and called out "Murder" '.

Next day, Cook refused to take any more medication. But Palmer had summoned Cook's own physician, Dr William Jones, from Lutterworth, and he, Bamford and Palmer persuaded the patient to take some pills made up by Dr Bamford. He agreed, not realizing that Bamford had given the pills to Palmer, who had bought more strychnine that morning, along with some prussic acid.

Cook's long ordeal was almost over. At midnight on Tuesday, the jangling bell in his room sent Elizabeth and her fellow chambermaid Lavinia Barnes hurrying upstairs. The patient was arched in excruciatingly painful contortions, resting only on his head and heels, as Dr Jones massaged his neck. Curiously, Cook was screaming for Palmer. One of the girls ran to the doctor's house, and found him fully dressed and ready. He forced two more pills through Cook's clenched teeth, and the poor man writhed in new agonies before slumping, lifeless, on the bed. The two chambermaids had watched the death scene in the errie candlelight with terrified awe. Now Elizabeth was amazed to see Palmer going through the dead man's pockets.

Desperation had forced the maniacal medic to throw all caution to the wind. he had already persuaded the Rugeley postmaster, Samuel Cheshire, to help him forge a cheque for £350 from Cook to Palmer. Now he asked him to witness a document saying Cook owed him another £4,000. Cheshire refused.

More trouble was in store for Palmer. On Friday, 23 November, Cook's stepfather, William Stevens, arrived in Rugeley. The appearance of the body, the haste with which it had been given to an undertaker, the search of Cook's pockets, and the claim for money from Cook's estate all made him suspicious. Unhappy with the stated cause of death, apoplexy, he ordered that the room where the body lay be locked, and left for London to see a solicitor, and demand a post-mortem.

It was held at the Talbot Arms on the following Monday morning, under the direction of a Dr Harland. Both Palmer and Bamford were present – one of the rare occasions a murderer has taken part in the search for clues to his murder. Palmer did all he could to obstruct that search. As the medical students cutting the body lifted out the stomach, Palmer brushed against them, and much of the vital contents spilled irretrievably back into abdomen. Harland reprimanded Palmer, assuming the doctor was playing a joke, and Palmer whispered to Bamford: 'They won't hang us yet.'

The stomach and intestines were sealed into a bottle, to be sent for analysis in

THE PRINCE OF POISONERS

London. Then the bottle disappeared. Harland angrily demanded to know where it was, and Palmer produced it from behind his back. There were two cuts in the air-proof lid. Still Palmer would not admit defeat. He offered the post-boy £10 if he would upset the carriage taking Stevens and the bottle to Stafford to catch the London train. The boy refused.

Palmer waited impatiently for the results of the London autopsy. He learned them before anyone else. Postmaster Cheshire was in the habit of allowing his friend to read any mail that interested him, and Palmer was delighted to intercept the report from the analyst. No poison had been found, apart from slight traces of antimony.

Palmer now took leave of his senses. He wrote two letters to the coroner, saying he was confident of a 'death by natural causes' verdict at the inquest – and enclosing the gift of some game and a £5 note. The coroner handed both letters and gifts to the police and recorded a verdict of wilful murder. Palmer, already in the custody of the sherrif's officer because of his debts, was arrested and taken to Stafford jail.

The bodies of his wife Ann and brother Walter were exhumed for post-mortems, and soon all England was talking of the Rugeley poisoner, attributing him with even more grisly deeds than those that were suspected. A special Act of Parliament, still known as 'Palmer's Law', had to be passed to transfer the trial from Stafford to the Old Bailey in London. Local prejudice was the given reason – and according to one of Palmer's defence team, Edward Kenealy, it was the fear that a local jury would never convict him. Kenealy wrote in his memoirs: 'Palmer was such a general favourite and had so many personal friends and acquaintances that no verdict of guilty could have been obtained.'

The Crown had no such problems at the Old Bailey. The trial, which began on 14 May, 1856, attracted intense attention from high society. The courtroom was packed each day, and outside throngs of spectators blocked the pavements to watch the protagonists arrive and leave. Bound volumes of verbatim evidence sold in their thousands, even though much of it was conflicting technical jargon from medical men.

The prosecution, led by Attorney-General Sir Alexander Cockburn made problems for itself by specifying that Cook was murdered by strychnine. Though Palmer was known to have bought it, no traces were found in Cook's corpse. Both sides brought in batteries of experts to try to explain this. Palmer's attorney, Serjeant Shee, berated one doctor for cruelty to animals after he spoke of the effects of strychnine on rabbits. Another man said the state of Cook's stomach when it reached London would have made establishing cause of death virtually impossible, 'if I had not been informed that there was a considerable quantity of strychnine present.'

Medical science knew little about the relatively new poison, or how to detect it, and some experts were prepared to swear that Palmer had found ways of disguising it. If so, he was not about to share the secret. There was little doubt that Palmer was guilty of poisoning Cook, and the jury and three judges were happy to go along with the Attorney-General's convenient theory: that Cook had been softened up with other poisons, then finished off by strychnine in an almost imperceptible dose. On 27 May, having listened to a masterly closing oration from Sir Alexander Cockburn, and a strong recommendation to convict from Lord Chief Justic Campbell, the jury took one hour to find Palmer guilty of murder.

He accepted sentence of death philosophically, and was taken back to Stafford under strong escort. He showed little sign of conscience or depression in prison, except when news that the Home Secretary had rejected his appeal came through, and to the end refused to make any confession, beyond saying, ambiguously: 'I am innocent of poisoning Cook by strychnine.'

Nearly 30,000 people were outside Stafford Jail on the morning of 14 June, 1856. Packed trains arrived in the town from the early hours, and spectators paid up to a guinea to take their places on the 23 platforms erected to give them a better view. When Palmer arrived, apparently indifferent to and amused by his fate, police had trouble controlling the mob as it surged forward. The sensational details of his sordid life had enthralled the nation, but there was nothing exceptional about his death at the end of the rope.

Few murderers have rivalled William Palmer for cold-hearted, premeditated callousness and cruelty. Though convicted and hanged for only one killing, he was suspected of at least 15 more, many of the victims being innocent children he fathered through debauched lechery. But even his horrific story has two wry postcripts. The moneylenders who hounded him received nothing after his death, because his mother refused to honour forged guarantees. And when the town of Rugeley, shamed by the notoriety brought on it by its infamous son, applied to change its name, the prime minister is alleged to have replied: 'By all means, provided you name your town after me.' His name was Lord Palmerston.

The Murderous Musician
CHARLES PEACE

What kind of man could sit calmly in a court's public gallery and watch another condemned to die for a murder he had committed? Charles Peace could. And it was only after his arrest, two years later, for another murder, that he made a full confession to a chaplain and saved the innocent prisoner's life. For stony-hearted Peace lived his criminal life by the maxim, 'If I make up my mind to a thing, I am bound to have it.' And for 20 years, he had made up his mind to be one of England's most cunning crooks.

Peace was a small, wiry man who walked with a limp and used an artificial hook arm to conceal the loss of two fingers in a childhood accident. He played the violin well enough to be billed at local concerts as 'The Modern Paganini'. But at night, he turned into an expert cat-burglar, carrying his tools in a violin case and using his monkey-like agility and phenomenal strength to plunder from the rooftops. For many years he wandered from town to town, until 1872, when he returned to his native Sheffield with his wife Hannah and their son Willie, and set up shop as a picture framer and bric-a-brac dealer in Darnall.

He was then 40, an ugly man whose tongue seemed too big for his mis-shaped mouth. Yet he seems to have had a way with certain women. He began an illicit affair with Mrs Katherine Dyson, the buxom wife of one of his neighbours in Britannia Road, visiting pubs to satisfy her craving for drink, then going to the attic of a nearby empty house to satisfy his own cravings. Soon Peace grew less cautious, calling on the Dysons whenever the fancy took him, and eventually Katherine's husband Arthur, a giant of over 2 metres in height, banned him from the house.

But Peace could not stand rebuffs. Mrs Dyson recalled later: 'I can hardly describe all that he did to annoy us . . . he would come and stand outside the window at night and look in, leering all the while. He had a way of creeping and crawling about, and of coming on you suddenly unawares.' The Dysons went to the police after their persecutor made threats at gunpoint in July 1876, but he fled to Hull to escape the arrest warrant that was issued. The Dysons decided to move home, to Banner Cross Terrace, Ecclesall Road, but when they arrived at what they thought would be their haven, Peace walked out of the front door, declaring: 'I am here to annoy you and I will annoy you wherever you go.'

On the evening of 29 November, Mrs Dyson left the house to visit the outside

WC. Peace was waiting in the shadows, holding a gun. Her shriek brought her husband running from the parlour, and he chased Peace down the alleyway that ran behind the terraced houses. When they reached the street, two shots were heard in rapid succession, and Dyson fell dying, a bullet in his head. Peace fled, dropping as he went a bundle of notes Mrs Dyson had written him. And though a reward of £100 was put on his head by police, he evaded capture, burgling his way from town to town until he reached London, and set up home in Evelina Road, Peckham.

It was a strange household. His wife Hannah and their son lived in the basement, while Peace and his mistress masqueraded as Mr and Mrs Thompson on the floor above, throwing musical parties for new friends and neighbours, and attending church every Sunday. Eventually the 'Thompsons' had a baby boy.

Peace cultivated a respectable image quite deliberately, saying: 'The police never think of suspecting anyone who wears good clothes.' He dyed his grey hair black, shaved off his beard. By day he drove his cart round south London, ostensibly collecting other people's unwanted possession. At night he went out and stole the possessions they were not so keen to lose. Though his exploits made the newspapers, police had no idea who the daring raider was, and Peace made the most of their ignorance. He delighted in chatting to policemen he met on trains, and even shared lodgings with an officer while staying briefly in Bristol.

But on 10 October, 1878, his luck ran out. Police were waiting in force outside a house in Blackheath when Peace emerged at 02.00 carrying a silver flask, a letter case and a cheque book. The cornered villain threatened them with a gun, and fired four shots, but the officers ignored him. The fifth shot struck PC Edward Robinson in the arm, but he still managed to overpower the gunman with colleagues, inflicting quite a beating-up in the process.

Peace was tried under the false name he gave, John Ward, for attempted murder, and the Old Bailey jury took four minutes to find him guilty. Despite a whining personal plea for mercy from the 'most wretched, miserable man,' he was jailed for life. Then his mistress revealed his true identity so she could collect the £100 murder reward still on offer at Sheffield. Police brought Mrs Dyson from her native America, where she had gone after the death of her husband, and charged Peace.

On 22 January, 1879, two warders accompanied the handcuffed prisoner on to the 05.00 express from London to Sheffield. He proved troublesome throughout the journey, and when the train reached Yorkshire, he flung himself out of a window. The warders stopped the train and ran back a mile to find him unconscious in the snow, having landed on his head. Committal proceedings were held outside his cell in Sheffield, and Peace was sent for trial at Leeds.

The jury took 12 minutes to find Peace guilty, and he was condemned to

Engraved portrait of Charles Peace at his trial

An artist's impression of Charles Peace escaping from the train

death. He spent the days before the execution writing moralistic letters and praying. And he also revealed to the chaplain, the Rev J. H. Littlewood, that four months before the death of Dyson he had shot and killed a policeman who disturbed him during a robbery at Whalley Range, Manchester.

Even more chillingly, he confessed that he had sat in the gallery at Manchester Assizes when two Irish brothers were charged with the death, and had watched 18-year-old William Habron be sentenced to death on 28 November just 24 hours before he shot Dyson. 'What man would have done otherwise in my position?' he said when asked why he had remained silent at such a blatant miscarriage of justice.

Habron was pardoned and given £800 compensation, and at 08.00 on 25 February, 1879, aged 46, Charles Peace took his place on the scaffold at Armley Jail, Leeds, after complaining bitterly about the 'bloody rotten bacon' he was served for his last breakfast. Though he pretended contrition and trust in God in an odious final speech, he confessed to the chaplain: 'My great mistake, sir, has been this: in all my career I have used ball cartridge; I ought to have used blank.' His last words before Marwood the executioner pulled the trapdoor lever were: 'I should like a drink; have you a drink to give me?' And he left his own epitaph in his cell. He was executed, he wrote, 'for what I done but never intended.'

The Triangular Chamber of Death

DR MARCEL PETIOT

Few mass killers have cashed in on the chaos of war as profitably as Dr Marcel Petiot. When the guillotine sliced his scheming head from his body on the morning of 26 May, 1946, he had made more than a million pounds from murder. And but for foolish pride, the 49-year-old doctor, might have escaped to enjoy his ill-gotten gains.

The medical profession was a natural choice of career for a man who showed sadistic tendencies even as a boy in his native Auxerre, where he relished cruelty to animals and smaller children. He spent World War One in a casualty clearing station at Dijon, peddling stolen morphia to drug addicts, before entering an asylum, where he studied medicine. By 1921 he had qualified as a doctor, and set up a practice in Villeneuve-sur-Yonne.

Flouting the Hippocratic oath, Petiot quickly prescribed a life of luxury for himself. He overcharged the rich while treating the poor for free. And villagers soon realized that Petiot was the man to see if they wanted drugs or illegal abortions. The mysterious disappearance of his young and pretty housekeeper when she became pregnant, and strange cries of pain from the good doctor's house, caused no more than idle gossip, and Petiot was soon sufficiently well-regarded to be elected Mayor.

But by 1930 life at Villeneuve had become too hot for him. One of his patients, a local shopkeeper, was robbed and killed, and Petiot was suspected, though nothing could be proved. Another patient persisted in accusing the doctor while continuing to visit him for treatment for his rheumatism. When he died suddenly, Petiot wrote 'natural causes' on the death certificate, and headed for bigger things in Paris.

Again his readiness to supply addictive drugs and terminate unwanted pregnancies soon earned him plenty of loyal patients. Quickly his practice at 60 Rue Caumartin became one of the most lucrative in the city. Petiot kept up the pretence of the good citizen – model husband and father, attending church each Sunday. His outward respectability helped him survive a fine for drug offences and the disappearance of a woman who unwisely accused him of turning her daughter into a junkie. Then, in 1940, the Nazi army marched into Paris. And Petiot seized the chance to set up a sinister sideline that satisifed both his passion for profits and his sadistic perversions.

THE TRIANGULAR CHAMBER OF DEATH

Dr Marcel Petiot, aged 49 in the Seine Assize Court

Gestapo activity had turned the French capital into a city of fear. Jews disappeared to concentration camp gas chambers, able-bodied Frenchmen were rounded up for labour camps, and those left behind soon learned that it did not pay to ask too many questions about friends who vanished. The situation was ideal for what Petiot had in mind.

He bought a disused mansion at 21 Rue Lesueur for half a million franc, then set about modifying it for his purposes. The house included a sound-proof triangular room with no windows and only one door. Petiot installed peepholes, telling the builders the room was for his mental patients. He installed a furnace in the cellar under the garage. Shortly before Christmas, 1941, everything was ready.

Petiot now spread the word that he was in touch with the French Resistance, and could smuggle people hunted by the Gestapo to safety in Spain or Cuba. The desperate refugees who contacted him were told that their escape would be costly, and that they would need innoculations before being allowed into their new lands. Such was their state of fear that they readily agreed, selling up all their possessions to meet the bills, or giving them to Petiot. One of the first customers, a Polish-born tailor, paid two million francs to get himself and his family out of France. One by one, they crept surreptitiously to Rue Lesueur, bared their arms for the necessary injections, and were ushered into the hidden triangular room. None of them left it alive.

When the doctor was satisfied, via his peepholes, that his deadly serum had done its work, he dragged the bodies to the cellar, where he treated them in quicklime – bought in bulk from his brother Maurice at Auxerre – before stuffing them into his grisly furnace. Then he scrupulously noted the details of each transaction – the money, jewellery, furs, gold and silver each victim had handed over.

As word spread, more and more customers queued at Petiot's door – Jews, people who had fallen foul of the Gestapo, rich families who were not prepared to wait until France was free of the Nazi terror. Petiot even dispatched a friend of his, Dr Paul Braumberger, a drug addict whose prostitute companion was appropriated by German troops, making it impossible for her earn the money to satisfy his cravings.

For 18 months, Petiot was able to combine curing patients at Rue Caumartin with killing them at Rue Lesueur. Though his wife noted how tired he was becoming, she never suspected the evil nature of his extra work.

But in the late spring of 1943, Petiot hit a snag. The Gestapo had been puzzled by the disappearance of several Jews they were seeking. When their investigations revealed that all had had links with Petiot they suspected he was what he pretended to be – a Resistance agent smuggling refugees to freedom. They sent a Gestapo man to Petiot, pleading to be sent abroad. Petiot had no reason to

Dr Marcel Petiot's execution

believe he was any different from his usual clients, and promptly killed him.

The Nazis arrested the doctor, and held him for several months before releasing him early in 1944. The suspicion was that Petiot had earned his freedom with one of the most bizarre defences ever – that he was only doing what the Germans were doing, killing Jews and anti-Nazis. However he had achieved it, he returned to his factory of death, and was soon busy burning bodies again.

Now, however, he had no way of treating them before throwing them into the flames. During his enforced absence, his brother Maurice had visited Paris, and called at the Rue Lesueur premises. Family loyalty and loathing for the Germans persuaded him to keep what he found there a grim secret, but he was no longer prepared to act as an accessory to disposing of human flesh, and cut off his supplies of quick lime.

Incinerating untreated remains made the smoke belching from Petiot's chimney even blacker and more acrid, and soon the doctor's neighbours, never happy about the pollution found it intolerable. On 11 March, 1944, the owner of 20 Rue Lesueur called both the police and fire brigade, saying the fumes were a fire danger. Petiot was not in, and a card on the door directed inquiries to his practice in Rue Caumartin. The gendarmes set off there while firemen broke in. They soon located the furnace, but what they found around it horrified them. Dismembered corpses littered the floor. Limbs, heads and torsos were scattered in grisly disarray. The firemen refused to do anything until the police returned.

Forensic experts later pieced together the bones and made a total of 27 human bodies. But when Petiot arrived, he blithely informed the gendarmes that all were Nazi collaborators who had betrayed the French maquis, and deserved the execution he had carried out. Amazingly, the police were prepared to give him at least some benefit of their doubt. Though still under the control of the Germans, they were Frenchmen who hoped the Allies would soon free them from Nazi oppression. They returned to HQ without Petiot.

The doctor was intelligent enough to know that the game was up. Once his story was checked, it would be obvious that he had lied. He fled Paris and for months laid low in the countryside. Meanwhile, senior police officers visited 21 Rue Lesueur, and discovered the cache of treasures, and Petiot's meticulous records. They showed that 63 people had entered the triangular room, never to leave it alive. And it was soon clear that none of them were traitors to France.

Far from being a patriot, Petiot was suspected of being a Gestapo agent. The front-page story of his horrific exploits stunned even a nation accustomed to Nazi atrocities. Yet the doctor declined to take his chance of disappearing in the confusion of the German retreat as the Allied armies reconquered France. He had talked his way out of so many awkward corners that he doubtless thought

THE TRIANGULAR CHAMBER OF DEATH

he could do it again. He wrote to the newspaper *Resistance*, claiming the Nazis had framed him by dumping bodies round the furnace while he was under arrest. Then he had the effrontery to enlist in the Free French forces under a false name.

As life returned to normal after the liberation, police began tidying up the loose ends of law and order. Petiot's case was a priority. Detectives guessed they had not seen the last of him, and they were right. When General de Gaulle led his army in a victory parade down the Champs Elysees, there was Petiot, marching proudly in rank with phoney medals on his chest. He had grown a beard, but he was wanted too badly to escape recognition.

Petiot insisted throughout his 18-month interrogation by a magistrate that he had killed only Germans and collaborators. But when he was brought to trial, the jury were not so gullible. They were shown 47 suitcases packed with more than 1,500 items of clothing, almost all without identity tags. They visited Petiot's triangular room, saw his cellar of death, and heard that he had plundered more than one million pounds from those he butchered.

When the verdict was announced, Petiot could not hear it above the excited babble of the court. He had to ask whether he had been found guilty or not. And when sentenced to death, he screamed: 'I will be avenged.' But he went to the guillotine quietly enough, leaving behind him an ironic epitaph to a blood-soaked life. He asked a companion on that final walk whether he could relieve himself. Permission was refused. Petiot was alleged to have joked: 'When one sets out on a voyage, one takes all one's luggage with one.' It was a luxury he did not allow any of his 63 victims.

The Teenage Monster

JESSE POMEROY

Horrified vacationers stumbled across the body of four-year-old Horace Millen on the beach at Dorchester Bay, near Boston, in April 1874. The child's throat has been cut and he had been stabbed no fewer than 15 times. Before he died, the boy had been savagely beaten. It was the work of a monster, and police immediately launched a full-scale hunt for the killer.

They were looking for a grown man, but some cross-referencing in the official files produced the name Jesse Harding Pomeroy: a lad of 14 who has been reprimanded and sent to a special reform school two years earlier for beating up young children. Fights among youngsters were commonplace, but the name of young Pomeroy, only just out of primary school, had been remembered by the authorities because of the extraordinary amount of unnecessary force he had used.

When police called on Jesse Pomeroy, his answers to questioning immediately aroused suspicion. He was arrested, brought to court and convicted. But Pomeroy's was one of the most remarkable murder cases ever. For, though sentenced to die, he was to live for another 58 years and the first 40 years – until he was 55 – were spent in solitary confinement.

The American public refused to take a chance on someone who had already displayed the most vicious cruelty. When arrested, he had been at liberty only 60 days after spending 18 months in the Westboro Reformatory. The magistrate who sent him there remarked on the savagery of the beatings he had handled out to children younger than himself and a short while after his trial for the Millen killing, it was established that just five weeks earlier he had killed nine-year-old Katie Curran. He had buried her body in the cellar of a shop.

At the Millen trial, Jesse Pomeroy pleaded innocence by way of insanity but it did him no good. He was convicted and sentenced to death. There were those who, because of his age, urged that his death sentence be commuted to life imprisonment but they were shouted down by the masses who demanded a swift execution. As it turned out, Pomeroy's life was spared only because of the legal complexities governing death sentences in the state of Massachusetts.

Although a judge had passed a sentence of death on him, the law required that the state governor of Massachusetts set the date of execution and sign the death warrant. Governor Gaston, in office at the time, refused possibly for political reasons to do anything at all: he would neither sign the death warrant nor commute young Pomeroy's sentence. He compromised with an order, signed and sealed, that Pomeroy must spend the rest of his natural days in solitary confinement. That order stood until long after Governor Gaston had passed away himself.

It was 1916, when Pomeroy was 54, before he was finally released from solitary and allowed to mix with other prisoners at Charlestown Prison. He had survived what must have been a superhuman ordeal by burying himself in studies. He read an immense number of books, and he wrote a lot himself.

If he had been mad at the time of the beatings, there was no longer any sign of it in his writings in these later years. One of the manuscripts he spawned was an autobiography which chronicled his early life, the crimes of which he had been convicted and an attempt he made to break out of jail.

Pomeroy died in the prison in which he had spent all his life, on 29 September, 1932. He was 73 and had spent more than 60 of those years behind bars.

The Suicide Murders

ROUSE, TETZNER, SAFFRAN AND KIPNIK

Over the years, many people have tried to evade their problems and responsibilities by disappearing, but three Europeans devized more fiendish means of vanishing. The men had never met, but within 12 months, each tried similar ways of escaping the mess they had made of their own lives – by taking the lives of complete strangers.

Alfred Arthur Rouse was known to his neighbours in Buxted Road, Finchley, London, as a cheery, chatty, charming chap. He and his wife Lily May had built a comfortable little home on the proceeds of his job as a commercial traveller for a Leicester company. Rouse loved his work. He was obsessed with cars, and had the gift of the gab when it came to selling.

Then, on 6 November, 1930, two plain clothes policemen called on Mrs Rouse. Her husband's Morris Minor car, registration number MU 1468, had been found burnt out in Hardingstone Lane, just off the London road near Northampton. A charred body had been found inside. Would she go with them to Northampton to try to identify some of the few personal effects left undamaged?

Mrs Rouse inspected some braces buckles and items of clothing, and thought they may have belonged to her husband. She was not allowed to see the corpse, which was virtually unidentifiable, but she was satisfied enough to start thinking of the £1,000 life insurance her husband had taken out on himself.

The police, however, were not so sure. Two young cousins, one of them the son of the village policeman at Hardingstone, had reported a strange encounter as they walked home from a 5 November Bonfire Night Party in Northampton. At 02.00, a car had flashed past them bound for London, and as they watched it, they saw a man scramble out of a roadside ditch. He was agitated and breathless, carrying an attache case and wearing a light raincoat, but no hat. As they wondered what he could be doing, they noticed a bright ball of flame 200 yards down Hardingstone Lane. The man said: 'It looks as if someone has had a bonfire.' But he went off in the opposite direction when the boys ran towards the blazing car.

That was enough to arouse police suspicions. What was a respectably-dressed man doing crawling about in a ditch at 02.00? Why did he not share the alarm

Alfred Rouse

Eight-year-old Fanny Adams was abducted while picking blackberries at Alton, Hampshire in 1867. Her dismembered body was found later that day. Her young killer was arrested and subsequently hanged. Sadly for Fanny's memory, the Royal Navy had just been issued with a new and unpalatable variety of canned meat which the sailors jokingly referred to as 'sweet Fanny Adams'. The phrase has since become part of the English language.

---

of the youngsters, and try to see if he could help fight the fire? They issued a nationwide alert for a man of between 30 and 35, about 2 metres (5ft 10in to 6ft) tall, with a round face and black curly hair. And at 21.20 on 7 November, they found him. Rouse was met by Scotland Yard detectives as he stepped from the Cardiff to London coach. And slowly they pieced together an amazing story of deception and callous cruelty.

Far from being a happily married suburban husband, Rouse was a bigamist. He had discovered that his good looks and amiable chat worked wonders with women, and he began to pick up waitresses and shop assistants on his travels.

In 1920, he made a 14-year-old Edinburgh girl pregnant. The child died after only five weeks, but Rouse persisted in the relationship, posing as a single man, and in 1924 went through a marriage ceremony with her at St Mary's Church, Islington, North London. A second child was born, and Rouse somehow persuaded her to let his real wife look after the boy from time to time in Buxted Road. In 1925, Rouse met a 17-year-old maid servant from Hendon, London, and was soon taking her with him on trips, and promising to marry her when trade picked up. She had a child by him in 1928, and gave birth to a second girl in October 1930 – seven days before he burnt his car. At the same time, a girl in the Monmouthshire village of Gellgaer was lying ill in her parents home. She too was pregnant by Rouse, and believed she was married to him. Rouse had promised her parents he had bought and furnished a house for him and his 'wife' at Kingston, and they would move there when the baby was born.

But the commercial traveller was earning only £10 a week. The new baby and the imminent one only added to his problems, which also included an illegitimate child in Paris and another in England. Rouse decided there was only one thing to do. He had to disappear, and start a new life, unfettered by responsibilities. A few days before the fateful 5 November, he met an unemployed man outside a public house in Whetstone, London. The man told him of his desperate hitch-hiking round the country in search of work, and added: 'I have no relations.' A fiendish idea came to Rouse as he noted that the man was about his own height and build.

THE SUICIDE MURDERS

On 5 November, Rouse visited the girl who had borne his daughter seven days earlier. She noticed that he seemed pre-occupied, constantly glancing at his watch. He left, muttering about bills he had to pay, and shortly after 20.00 met the unemployed man by arrangement in Whetstone High Road. He had promised to drive him to Leicester in search of a job.

Rouse was a teetotaller, but he brought along a bottle of whisky for his new friend, and the man drank from it liberally. Near St Albans, the inebriate switched off the car lights by mistake, and they were stopped by a policeman, but allowed to drive on after a warning. What happened next was told with chillingly clinical efficiency in a confession Rouse wrote just before his execution.

'He was the sort of man no-one would miss, and I thought he would suit the plan I had in mind,' he wrote. 'He drank the whisky neat from the bottle and was getting quite fuzzled. We talked a lot, but he did not tell me who he actually was. I did not care.

I turned into Hardingstone Lane because it was quiet and near a main road where I could get a lift from a lorry afterwards. I pulled the car up. The man was half-dozing – the effect of the whisky. I gripped him by the throat with my right hand. I pressed his head against the back of the seat. He slid down, his hat falling off. I saw he had a bald patch on the crown of his head.

He just gurgled. I pressed his throat hard. The man did not realize what was happening. I pushed his face back. After making a peculiar noise, the man was silent. I got out of the car, taking my attache case, a can of petrol and a mallet. I walked about eight metres (ten yards) in front of the car and opened the can, using the mallet to do so. I threw the mallet away and made a trail of petrol to the car. Also I poured petrol over the man and loosened the petrol union joint and took the top off the carburettor. I put the petrol can in the back of the car.

I ran to the beginning of the petrol trail and put a match to it. The flame rushed to the car, which caught fire at once. Petrol was leaking from the bottom of the car. That was the petrol I had poured over the man and the petrol that was dripping from the union joint and carburettor. The fire was very quick and the whole thing was a mass of flames in a few seconds. I ran away.'

In fact Rouse had planned the killing flawlessly. The left leg of the unconscious man was doubled up under the leaking union joint, so that the constant drip would send intense heat into the victim's face, making it unrecognizable. The man's right arm was stretched towards the can in the back seat, and soaked to produce another source of flames to the head and shoulders. And though he had tampered with the engine, the damage was consistent with what might be expected in an accidental blaze.

But the calculating killer had not reckoned on meeting two witnesses as he ran away. And it was that which proved his undoing. Knowing he had been seen, he panicked. Instead of escaping to a new life, he hitched a lift home to Finchley in a lorry, arriving at 06.20. He stayed only to change his clothes, then took a coach to Cardiff and Gellygaer. All the way, he unnecessarily told people his car had been stolen, but changed the details each time. To his amazement, the story of the burned-out car was on the front page of every newspaper. People who knew him in Gellygaer kept asking if it was his car. He denied it, and decided to return to London. Waiting for the coach in Cardiff, he again told conflicting tales about how his car had gone missing. He seemed almost relieved to be met at Hammersmith by the police.

But his horrific confession was still many months away. He first claimed that he had picked the man up as a hitch-hiker near St Albans, then lost his way. When the engine started to spit, he stopped to relieve himself, and told the passenger to fill the tank from his petrol can. The man asked for a cigarette. Next thing, Rouse claimed, he turned and saw a ball of flame. He ran back to the car, but could not get near it because of the heat. Then he had 'lost his head' after coming over 'all of a shake', and had fled, feeling vaguely responsible but not knowing what to do.

It was a plausible story, and though Rouse changed certain details in subsequent re-tellings of it, he still arrived at Northampton Assizes with a jaunty, self-assured air on 26 January, 1931. The prosecution, led by Norman Birkett, had a tricky task to prove murder, and Rouse knew it.

Unfortunately for him, his confidence was his undoing. Rouse had been invalided out of World War One with head wounds after a shell exploded close to where he was standing in the trenches at Givenchy, northern France. A medical report on him in September 1918 said: 'The man is easily excited and talkative.' That, as much as the chance meeting in the country lane, was to condemn him to the noose.

When Birkett suggested Rouse had thrown the man into the car carelessly, face down, Rouse was foolish enough to argue that he had more brains than to do that. Another witness, an expert on car fires, noticed that Rouse seemed unperturbed, even amused, while the court discussed whether the carburettor top might have melted or fallen off. Rouse was also too keen to offer technical explanations about what might have happened inside the blazing engine. He was too clever by half.

The most damning evidence was produced by the eminent pathologists Sir Bernard Spilsbury and Dr Eric Shaw. They testified that the victim had been unconscious but alive when the fire began, and that a tiny scrap of unburnt clothing from the crotch of his trousers was soaked in petrol. Other expert witnesses contended that the man could have spilled petrol over himself, but

The burned-out car containing Rouse's victim

they did not carry much weight with a jury who looked on appalled at an accused man who coldly discussed leaving his 'good wife' because she never made a fuss of him, inexplicably made no real effort to rescue the man in his car, and, worst of all, never showed the slightest compassion or concern for the unknown wretch who had died.

On 31 January, 1931, Mr Justice Talbot sentenced Alfred Arthur Rouse, one of the most ingenious yet most loathsome murderers in British criminal history, to death. His appeal against sentence was dismissed 23 days later, and on 10 March Rouse was hanged at Bedford.

A week later, Kurt Erich Tetzner, also a young commercial traveller, stepped into the dock at Ratisbon, Germany, accused of burning to death in his car an unknown man with intent to defraud insurance companies by passing the body off as his own.

Tetzner had been in custody for 14 months, having been arrested ten days after his burnt-out car was found on the outskirts of Etterhausen, Bavaria, on 25 November, 1929. The charred body at the wheel was buried in lavish style by a weeping Frau Tetzner, who had identified it as her husband, but police were alerted by insurance companies who stood to pay out nearly £7,500. They watched the widow take two telephone calls at a neighbour's house from a Herr Stranelli in Strasbourg, Alsace, and soon discovered that Stranelli and Tetzner were the same man.

Tetzner was worse than Rouse at explaining his crime. He admitted the insurance fraud, and at first confessed to murdering the passenger. But five months after his arrest, he changed his story, saying the man in the car was a pedestrian he had run over who had died as he took him to hospital.

The court found it inconceivable that anyone would confess to murder to try to cover up a case of manslaughter. And it doubted the second story after Tetzner made another admission. Once he had advertised for a travelling companion, but the man who answered dropped out. The second time, he had attacked his passenger, a motor mechanic called Alois Ortner, with a hammer and a pad of ether, after first giving him money to make himself look respectable by having a shave and buying a collar. But Ortner had proved too strong for him and escaped into a nearby forest. Ortner was called as a prosecution witness, and revealed that he had gone to police after the attack – but they refused to believe his 'fantastic' story.

Tetzner was condemned to death, and the sentence was carried out on 2 May, 1931. Shortly before, the young murderer at last confessed the truth. He had picked up an unknown young man in thin clothes who complained of being cold. Tetzner wrapped a rug around him, trapping his arms, then strangled him with rope. He then crashed the car into a tree, made a petrol trail and set fire to it.

THE SUICIDE MURDERS

The public prosecutor at Ratisbon referred to Rouse as 'just a pupil of Tetzner.' It is not known whether Rouse had heard of the German case before he hatched his own scheme. But the third man who tried to disappear by substituting another man's body for his own certainly had.

Fritz Saffran was young, good-looking and successful. He had made such a good job of running the Platz Furniture Store in Rastenburg, eastern Prussia, that the owner of the shop, whose daughter he married, felt able to retire early, and leave things to his 30-year-old son-in-law.

Then, on 15 September 1930, an explosion rocked the store, and flames quickly destroyed it. Thirty workers escaped, but one did not. Chief clerk Erich Kipnik claimed Saffran had dashed into the blazing building to try to save the ledgers. Sure enought, firemen sifting the debris found the charred body. It wore the remains of one of Saffran's suits, had two of his rings on its fingers, and his monogrammed watch in an inside pocket.

Saffran had been popular with all his staff and customers, but one employee in particular was inconsolable at his death. It was known that Ella Augustin had been in love with him for years, but that he had publicly refused to respond to her flirting. He was, after all, a happily married man.

Two days after the fire, Ella called at several garages in the town to try to hire a car to take her mother, who was seriously ill, to Konigsberg. The chauffeur who accepted the task was surprised to be asked to arrive at her house at 03.00. He was even more amazed when the ailing mother turned out to be Saffran.

The man drove to the village of Gerdauen, but refused to go further. He had worked for the Platz firm before, and was reluctant to go to the police. But he told a friend about the secret journey, and was arrested – though later cleared – for aiding Saffran's escape. The friend alerted the police, who quickly discovered that all was not what it seemed at the prosperous Platz store. Saffran had burdened the business with huge debts after hire purchase buyers defaulted on payments. He had also raised money fraudulently on fake hire purchase deals and falsified the ledgers. Ella Augustin had helped him do this, and was his secret lover.

Greedy Mongol Tamerlane the Great was feared as much by his own men as by his enemies. After one battle, he built pyramids out of layer upon layer of murdered prisoners' heads. And if anyone dared to tell a joke in his company, they would be instantly killed. He died after a month of gluttony in 1405.

THE WORLD'S MOST INFAMOUS MURDERS

> **The seventeenth-century Tsar of Russia, Peter the Great, murdered his own son when he remonstrated with him about his cruel laws. Anyone who opposed this giant of over 2 metres in height suffered a chilling death. His mistress, a Scot named Mrs Hamilton, was unfaithful to him – so he pickled her head and placed it beside his bed.**

She was arrested, and tried to smuggle a note out to Saffran. It told the police that he was staying with one of her relatives in Berlin. Saffran somehow learned that police in the German capital were looking for him. Seven weeks after his getaway he stole the relative's identity papers, took a local train to the suburb of Spandau, and boarded the 01.00 train to Hamburg, where he hoped to get a ship to Brazil. But a fluke thwarted his clever plans. The rail official at Spandau had lived in Rastenburg several years earlier, and recognized the fugitive. Police were waiting when the train pulled into Wittenburg, the next station down the line.

Dental records helped detectives identify the body in the Platz store as Friedrich Dahl, 25, a dairyman from Wermsdorf, near Konigsberg. And on 23 March, 1931, Saffran and Kipnik, arrested when he was implicated in the conspiracy, went on trial at Bartenstein charged with Dahl's murder, attempted murder, arson, forgery, bribery and insurance frauds. Ella Augustin was accused of incitement to murder and complicity in frauds.

It quickly became clear that all three were more than anxious to blame each other for the murder. And what emerged was a chilling story of cold, calculated killing. Ella claimed that Saffran started it, brandishing a newspaper and saying: 'Have you read the report about this man Tetzner? That is how I will do our job too.'

Saffran claimed he took out an insurance policy for £7,000 so his wife would be well provided for. It was his intention to commit suicide, but Ella argued him out of it. Kipnik then suggested securing a body and burning it. They considered digging up a corpse from a grave, but dismissed the idea as impractical for their purposes.

The court was hushed as Saffran continued: 'We established a murder camp in the Nikolai Forest. The girl stayed there while Kipnik and I, each in his own car, roved the countryside for miles around, looking for a likely victim, then reported to the camp at evening. After a while we all three began to go out on these manhunts together.'

Several countrymen had lucky escapes. Once, near the village of Sorquitten, a man accepted a lift. Saffran said he speeded up, then jammed on the brakes, and Kipnik was supposed to smash the victim's skull as it jolted back. But Ella lost her nerve, clutched Kipnik's arm, and the man got away.

Kipnik claimed that, on another occasion, they picked up a pedestrian and were about to kill him when he revealed that he had six children. Sometimes they hid in woods or behind hedges, waiting for a likely victim to come along. The search went on night after night. Finally, on 12 September, 1930, Kipnik and Saffran met a man near Luisenhof just about midnight. It was Dahl.

Both men accused the other of firing the fatal three shots into his head, and both made exaggerated claims of contrition when the victim's widow took the stand. The public prosecutor had to tell them sternly to stop play-acting. But both continued to speak in terms more suited to a playhouse than a courtroom. 'Gentlemen of the jury, think of my terrible position,' Saffran pleaded, arms outstretched. 'I was leading a double life. At home I had to appear cheerful and contented while my heart was breaking. At night I was forced to go out hunting for men to murder.' Later Kipnik shouted: 'Saffran has ruined my life. I place my fate in the hands of the court. I wish I could prove to them that I am really a decent man.'

The jury believed neither story, and both men were sentenced to death. Accomplice Ella was jailed for five years. But Saffran and Kipnik were luckier than Rouse and Tetzner. The Prussian government commuted their sentences to life imprisonment. Many Germans wondered why two such callous killers should be spared the fate they had so cold-bloodedly meted out to an innocent stranger.

The Rat Poisoner

LYDIA SHERMAN

Wherever Lydia Sherman went she found buildings infested with rats. Or at least that was the story she told the neighborhood druggists from whom she bought her poison.

The arsenic soon eliminated the rats and, as it turned out, some of the human beings she considered a nuisance, too. As many as 42 people are believed to have died by Lydia's hand.

Married to patrolman Edward Struck of the New York Police Department, the sturdy but attractive housewife kept a low profile until 1864. Then Struck was sacked by the police for a shabby display of cowardice and promptly turned into an unemployed drunk. Lydia put him to bed one evening with a lethal snack of oatmeal gruel and rat poison.

Puzzled as to the manner of his death, the doctor blamed it on 'consumption' but made up his mind to ask for an official investigation. But Lydia had ensured her husband had a quick burial and the authorities saw no reason to intrude on her 'grief'.

One by one Lydia's children died – Mary Ann, Edward, William, George, Ann Eliza, and finally the widow's namesake, tiny toddler Lydia. In every case she shrewdly called in a different doctor, all of whom obligingly took her word for the cause of death.

When the people of San José, California, heard the fate of local kidnap victim Brooke Hart, they decided to seek vengeance. In 1933, Brooke Hart, a 22-year-old heir to a hotel chain, was kidnapped by garage worker Thomas Thurmond and his old schoolfriend John Holmes. The pair attacked him with a brick, weighted him down and threw him into the sea. To their amazement Hart came to and began yelling, so they shot him.

Thurmond and Holmes demanded $40,000 from Hart's father for the 'safe return' of his son. But the police traced the kidnappers' phone calls and the evil couple were arrested. When Brooke Hart's body was discovered, a raging mob broke into Santa Clara Jail, put out one of Holmes' eyes and then hung him and Thurmond from nearby trees.

THE RAT POISONER

An ex-brother-in-law went to the authorities swearing Lydia was 'full of black evil' and demanding that the bodies be exhumed. But the bored bureaucrats refused to budge.

Lydia moved from one job to another. In 1868 she married an aging and rich widower named Dennis Hurlbut. With rat poison available at 10 cents a package, he was soon out of the way.

That left her free to marry Nelson Sherman, who took her with him to his Connecticut home. There she had problems, including a suspicious mother-in-law and the four Sherman children by a previous marriage.

Two of the children she disposed of at once. Mourning the death of his 14-year-old daughter, Addie, Nelson Sherman turned to alcohol and thus signed his own death warrant.

'I just wanted to cure him of the liquor habit,' Lydia said.

A Connecticut doctor was suspicious and insisted that his stomach and liver be analyzed. Toxicologists found enough arsenic to kill an army. The vital organs of the two children were also permeated with poison.

Pleading that she had murdered out of human compassion – 'all those people were sick, after all' – the fashionably dressed widow cut an impressive figure at her trial in New Haven, Connecticut. And in a way, her luck held. Amazingly gentle with the not so gentle murderess, Judge Park instructed the jury to consider only charges of second-degree murder.

Sentenced to life in Weathersfield Prison, she vowed she would never die in jail. But there her luck did end – she was still behind bars when she died in 1878.

The Yorkshire Ripper

PETER SUTCLIFFE

When the savagely-mutilated body of Wilma McCann, a 28-year-old prostitute, was found on 30 October, 1975, on playing fields in Leeds, no-one but the police took much notice. The newspapers dismissed her murder with a few paragraphs, and her neighbours, while shocked by the tragedy, explained that 'Hotpants' McCann was 'no better than she ought to have been'.

Only Wilma's four children and a handful of friends mourned her wretched end. The honest citizens of Leeds, long angered by the vice which flourished in the Chapeltown district where Wilma lived, quickly forgot about her death.

However, Dennis Hoban, the 48-year-old head of Leeds area CID could not forget the horrific injuries he had seen on McCann's body – the skull smashed in with a blunt instrument, the trunk punctured by 15 stab wounds. 'The attack was savage and frenzied,' Chief Superintendent Hoban told a press conference. 'It suggested the work of a psychopath and, with this kind of person, there is always the likelihood that he will strike again.' His words were grimly prophetic.

During the next five years the man who came to be known as 'the Yorkshire Ripper' struck many times, killing 12 more women and maiming seven – a terrifying, shadowy figure who brought near hysteria to the cobbled streets of West Yorkshire and who sparked off the biggest police hunt of the century.

His grim nickname, reminiscent of London's Jack the Ripper of 1888, did not hit the headlines until his second murder – that of part-time prostitute Mrs Emily Jackson, 42, in a Chapeltown alleyway on 20 January, 1976 – less than three months after the McCann killing.

Mrs Jackson's body, too, was dreadfully mutilated. Repeated blows from a blunt instrument had stove in the back of the skull and the bloodstained trunk was punctured by 50 cruciform-shaped stab wounds, caused by a sharpened Phillip's-type screwdriver.

Chief Superintendent Hoban appealed to the public: 'I can't stress strongly enough that it is vital we catch this brutal killer before he brings tragedy to another family.'

If the first murder had been virtually ignored, the second was given big play by the press. And it was George Hill, of the *Daily Express* who coined the soubriquet 'the Yorkshire Ripper'.

Wilma McCann

Emily Jackson

Joan Harrison

Irene Richardson

On 8 February, 1977, the Ripper killed again. His victim, another prostitute, was 28-year-old Irene Richardson, whose stabbed body was found in Roundhay Park, Leeds. Although Roundhay is a highly-respectable, middle-class suburb, it is little more than a mile from the edge of the Chapeltown district where McCann and Jackson had died.

Less than three months later the Ripper's grim 'score' rose to four and, once again, the victim was a prostitute, Tina Atkinson, aged 32, who was found battered to death on 24 April. She was on the bed of her flat in the Lumb Lane area of Bradford, a 'red light' district smaller than Leeds's Chapeltown, but with an equally bad reputation.

As in the three previous killings, the Ripper had left precious few clues for the police beyond his 'trademark' of hammerblows to the skull. Of the few clues, however, one was vital: the footprint made by a boot, which exactly matched a print found at the scene of Emily Jackson's murder.

It was a useful break for the weary and bewildered CID men, but they were still being hampered by lack of public concern. What they needed was something that would bring forward witnesses who, up to then, had refused to get involved on the grounds that the victims were 'only prostitutes'.

They got what they wanted on the morning of Sunday 26 June, 1977, but there was not a policeman in the West Yorkshire force who did not wish that it could have happened some other way.

Jayne MacDonald was found battered and stabbed to death in a children's playground in the heart of Chapeltown. But Jayne, just 16, blonde and with filmstar good looks, was no prostitute – just a happy teenager, ruthlessly cut down by the Ripper while walking home after a night out with a boyfriend. Now, at last, after almost two years of working against public apathy, the police had an 'innocent' victim on their hands.

From that moment there was no shortage of information. On the contrary, the Ripper Squad began slowly to founder under the weight of facts, theories and suppositions from the general public.

There is no doubt that the slaying of Jayne MacDonald led to the death of her father, railwayman Wilf MacDonald, two years later. Soon after Jayne's killing he told reporters how his daughter had bent to kiss him on the head before going out on that fateful night. 'She was so sweet and clean,' said Mr MacDonald. 'She was untouched and perfect, just like a flower.'

The next time he saw her was on a mortuary slab. He said: 'The pain of seeing her blonde hair, which had been so shiny and clean the night before, now caked in blood was so indescribable it haunts my every waking moment.'

From that moment Wilf MacDonald waited for death, praying for the moment when he would be released from the horror that the Ripper had visited upon him. When he died broken-hearted on 11 October, 1979, he was a Ripper

Patricia Atkinson

Jayne MacDonald

Jean Jordan

Yvonne Pearson

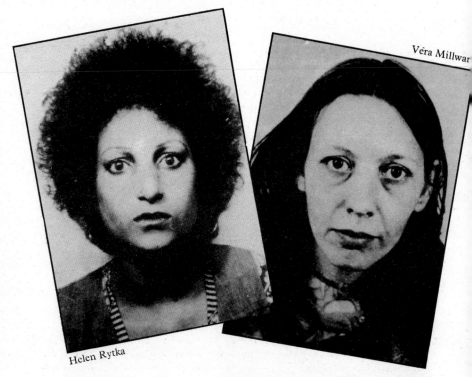

Vera Millward

Helen Rytka

victim just as surely as if he had been killed by a blow from a ball-pein hammer.

By then six more women had been murdered: Jean Jordan, aged 21, prostitute, murdered and hideously mutilated on allotments in Manchester, on 1 October, 1977. Yvonne Pearson, aged 22, prostitute, murdered on 21 January, 1978, on waste ground in Bradford. Her badly decomposed body was not found until 26 March. Helen Rytka, aged 18, prostitute, murdered beneath a railway viaduct in Huddersfield, West Yorkshire, on 31 January 1978. Vera Millward, aged 41, prostitute, murdered in the grounds of Manchester Royal Infirmary on 17 May, 1978. Josephine Whitaker, aged 19, a respectable building society clerk, bludgeoned to death near her home in Halifax, Yorkshire, while taking a short cut through Savile Park on the night of 4 April, 1979. Barbara Leach, aged 20, a respectable student at Bradford University, killed near Bradford city centre in the early hours of 2 September, 1979.

Three months before the slaying of 'Babs' Leach, a sensational twist to the Ripper inquiry had echoed all round the world, giving newspapers, television and radio one of the most bizarre crime stories ever to hit the headlines. It was in the form of a cassette tape, played at a press conference on 26 June by Assistant Chief Constable George Oldfield, head of West Yorkshire CID.

'I'm Jack,' said the voice on the tape in a chilling monotone. 'I see you are still having no luck catching me. I have the greatest respect for you, George, but, Lord, you are no nearer catching me than four years ago when I started. I reckon your boys are letting you down, George. you can't be much good, can ya? The only time they came near catching me was a few months back in Chapeltown when I was disturbed. Even then it was a uniform copper, not a detective.

I warned you in March that I'd strike again. Sorry it wasn't Bradford. I did promise you that, but I couldn't get there. I'm not quite sure when I will strike again, but it will be definitely some time this year, maybe September or October, even sooner if I get the chance. I am not sure where, maybe Manchester. I like it there, there's plenty of them knocking about. They never learn, do they, George. I bet you've warned them, but they never listen.

At the rate I'm going I should be in the book of records. I think it's up to eleven now, isn't it. Well, I'll keep on going for quite a while yet. I can't see myself being nicked just yet. Even if you do get near I'll probably top myself first.

'Well, it's been nice chatting to you, George. Yours, Jack the Ripper.

No good looking for fingerprints. You should know by now it's as clean as a whistle. See you soon. Bye. Hope you like the catchy tune at the end. Ha. Ha. Ha.'

The music that followed was the six-line reprise of 'Thank You For Being a Friend', a 1978 song by Californian musician Andrew Gold.

As the music faded, George Oldfield said: 'I believe that we have now got the break we have been waiting for.'

But that was where it all started to go wrong. The Ripper inquiry went off course at a tragic tangent. For the voice on the tape was identified by dialect experts as belonging to someone from the Castletown district of Sunderland. From that moment detectives manning the £4,000,000 hunt for the Ripper began looking for a man with a Geordie accent. . .

Peter William Sutcliffe did not have a Geordie accent. His voice, slightly high-pitched and hesitant, was flat with the broad vowels of his native town of Bingley, a few miles to the west of Bradford.

There, on the fringes of the Brontë country, Sutcliffe was born on 2 June, 1946, the first child of John and Kathleen Sutcliffe who lived in a one-up, one-down cottage in Heaton Row, close by the edge of the wild moors above Bingley.

Peter was a shy boy, prone to blushing in the company of girls, though his polite good manners were much admired by his parents' neighbours. He left

Cottingley Manor School, Bingley, at the end of spring term in 1961, aged 15, and for three years drifted through a variety of undistinguished jobs before starting work as a gravedigger in Bingley Cemetery in 1964. With the exception of a short break in 1965, he remained at the job until he was sacked for bad timekeeping in 1967 . . . and loved every minute of it.

Sutcliffe's gravedigging career is littered with revolting stories of desecration and grave-robbing that tell of the dark shadows that were already gathering in his mind. Often he outraged his workmates by interfering with corpses, sometimes to steal rings or gold teeth, but other times simply because he seemed to enjoy handling dead bodies.

Eventually he managed to get himself attached to the mortuary as an attendant and would regale his friends with descriptions of the cadavers he had seen cut open for post-mortem examination. Often, after a night in the pub, he would rattle the mortuary keys and ask if anyone wanted to see the latest body. There were never any takers.

Sutcliffe was married on 10 August, 1974, at Clayton Baptist Chapel, Bradford. It was a double celebration for that day was also the birthday of his bride, Sonia Szurma, an attractive 24-year-old teacher, daughter of eastern European refugees. A shy girl, Sonia looked even more demure than usual at her wedding. She could not have known that her groom had ended the previous evening's stag night celebrations by taking himself down to Bradford's red light district of Lumb Lane. But the darkly-handsome, sallow-faced Sutcliffe was a frequent visitor to Lumb Lane, and to Leeds's Chapeltown, and to Manchester's Moss Side.

Fourteen months after marrying Sonia, Sutcliffe killed Wilma McCann, and those infamous districts became a slaughterhouse where women lived in terror and police sought desperately for a murderer with a Geordie accent.

They had one gift of a clue – a brand new £5 note found in the handbag of the Ripper's first Manchester victim, Jean Jordan, murdered on 1 October, 1977. The serial number, AW51 121565, was traced to the Midland Bank at Shipley, a suburb of Bradford. The manager explained to detectives that the note had been issued only five days before it had been handed over to Jordan – probably in the pay-roll of a local firm.

Manchester police sent a team over to Shipley to join their West Yorkshire colleagues, and thousands of local men were interviewed. Among them was the entire workforce of T. and W. H. Clark, an engineering and haulage firm, based in Canal Road, Shipley.

One of the men interviewed was a lorry driver called Sutcliffe. In the cab of his lorry was pinned this handwritten notice: 'In this truck is a man whose latent genius, if unleashed, would rock the nation, whose dynamic energy would overpower those around him. Better let him sleep.'

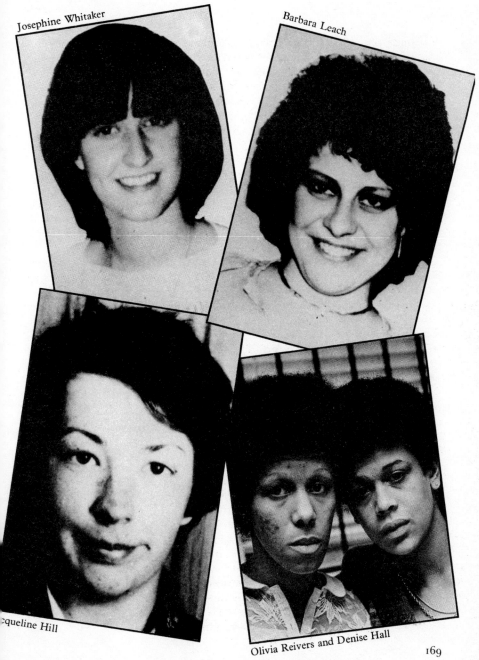

Josephine Whitaker

Barbara Leach

cqueline Hill

Olivia Reivers and Denise Hall

If the detectives trying to trace the owner of the £5 note saw the notice they did not read any significance into it for Peter Sutcliffe was questioned and cleared.

He was to be interviewed another eight times throughout the remaining span of the Ripper enquiry . . . and each time he was cleared and released. His workmates at Clark's even joked about the number of times he was questioned and gave him the nickname 'the Ripper'.

By now, under the influence of the intelligent, well-educated Sonia, Sutcliffe was busy bettering himself. Always immaculately dressed in crisp, fresh overalls, he had a reputation as one of Clark's top drivers. And he and Sonia moved into the decidedly middle-class Heaton district of Bradford, buying a four-bedroomed detached house in Garden Lane.

But strange things happened behind the respectable lace curtains at Number 6. There was domestic friction with the tiny, frail Sonia often heard ranting and shouting at her embarrassed husband, ignoring his pleas to keep her voice down 'in case the neighbours hear'.

It is a bizarre concept – the monstrously evil killer as a henpecked husband, but in Sutcliffe's case it was true. More than one detective on the Ripper Squad has said: 'Every time he killed, he was really killing Sonia.'

The faithful and devoted husband, the loyal and hardworking employee, the polite and helpful friend, these were the faces that Peter Sutcliffe showed to the rest of the world. The face of the fiend was one he reserved for darkness – and his victims. At first they had been prostitutes and, in a perverted way, he could try to justify their deaths, as did the original Jack the Ripper, by claiming that he was ridding the streets of 'filth'.

But then had come the murder of Jayne MacDonald. She had been no whore. Nor had Jo Whitaker or Babs Leach, victims number ten and eleven. Nor had several of the women who had survived his attacks. So now there could be no pretence of being a crusading 'street-cleaner'.

Was he seeking to punish the domineering Sonia? Or was he seeking revenge on all womankind? For in 1972 Sutcliffe, his two sisters and two brothers, had been astounded and horrified to discover that their mother, Kathleen, the woman they called 'the Angel', had been having a secret affair. Highly religious, even prudish, Kathleen had slipped from the pedestal on which her doting children had placed her.

Perhaps it is significant that the twelfth victim was, like the late Mrs Sutcliffe (she died in November 1978), middle-aged and highly respectable. Margo Walls was 47, a former sergeant in the WRAC, an unmarried civil servant who lived alone in Pudsey, a small town between Leeds and Bradford.

After working late on 22 August, 1980, she set off to walk the half mile from her office to her home – and met Sutcliffe. He reared out of the dark shadows of a gateway and aimed a blow at her head. Although stunned, Miss Walls fought

Peter Sutcliff and Sonia on their wedding day

Peter Sutcliffe's fantasy woman, Theresa Douglas

back savagely, punching and clawing at her attacker. But the slightly built Sutcliffe was strong and managed to get a garotte around her neck. When Margo was dead, Sutcliffe stripped her body, dragged her up the driveway – that of a local magistrate – and buried her beneath a pile of grass cuttings.

Police investigating the murder decided that it was not the work of the Ripper. The garotte, they said, was not his style. But three months later, on Monday 17 November, 1980, the Ripper struck again and this time there was no doubt in the minds of the investigating detectives.

The victim was Jacqueline Hill, a 20-year-old student at Leeds University. At 21.23 that fateful Monday night she alighted from a bus outside the Arndale shopping centre in the residential district of Headingley, Leeds, and began walking the 200 metres up Alma Road towards her hall of residence.

Sutcliffe, who minutes before had been eating chicken and chips from a nearby Kentucky Fried Chicken shop, leapt out of his parked Rover and rained hammerblows on the back of her head. She went down without a sound, laying limply as her attacker dragged her across Alma Road into some bushes behind the Arndale Centre. There, with a sharpened screwdriver, he set about inflicting his terrible trademark on her body. The final wound was the worst of all – a stab through the retina of the eye 'because', Sutcliffe explained after his arrest, 'she seemed to be staring at me.'

The killing of yet another respectable victim, particularly in the straight-laced heart of middle-class Headingley, caused a more violent eruption of public fury and indignation than before. West Yorkshire's Chief Constable, Mr Ronald Gregory, was being pressed hard by the public and local politicians who demanded action fast.

On 25 November he announced the formation of a 'super squad' – a think-tank of senior officers drawn from other forces. Assistant Chief Constable George Oldfield was, effectively, taken off the case, although he remained head of West Yorkshire CID.

It must have been a bitter blow for Oldfield who had lived, day and night, with the case almost from the start. The hunt for the Ripper had become a personal crusade, especially since that tape recording had arrived to taunt him.

In his place, with the temporary acting rank of Assistant Chief Constable, Mr Gregory appointed Jim Hobson, head of Leeds area CID, successor to Chief Superintendent Dennis Hoban who had begun the inquiry and who had died suddenly at the age of 51 in March 1978.

Hobson and Oldfield did not see eye to eye. Their relationship was correct rather than cordial and Hobson lost no time in getting rid of the albatross of the 'Geordie accent' that had hung round the neck of the inquiry for so long. Oldfield, who had virtually staked his reputation on the tape, could only watch.

Then Hobson, in a statement that was almost clairvoyant, announced that if the Ripper was caught 'it will be by an ordinary uniformed copper, going about his normal duties'.

That is exactly what happened on the night of Friday, 2 January, 1981, as Peter Sutcliffe prepared to kill his fourteenth victim – a coloured Sheffield prostitute called Ava Reivers. The two of them were sitting in Sutcliffe's Rover V8 in the driveway of an office block in Melbourne Drive, Sheffield. Sutcliffe had handed over a £10 note for sex, but had failed to get an erection. On the back seat were a hammer, a garotte and a sharpened screwdriver.

The man who had called himself 'Dave' suddenly whispered to Ava: 'I'm scared – really scared.' But it was Ava who was scared; somehow she knew beyond doubt that this 'punter' intended her harm.

At that moment the police arrived, a sergeant and a PC in a panda car, making a routine check on the cars parked in the leafy lovers' lane. 'Dave' was reduced to near panic.

Ava, pleased for the first time in her life to see a policeman, was relieved to be taken to the police station for questioning about her 'lover's' identity and for him to be quizzed as to why the Rover was carrying false number plates.

It was during that interview that Sergeant Arthur Armitage, after studying the man who claimed to be 'Peter Williams', suddenly spoke up. In his broad South Yorkshire accent he said: 'Tha's t' Ripper, thee!'

The nightmare was over.

On Friday, 22 May, 1981, Peter William Sutcliffe stood in the dock at the Old Bailey's Number One court and listened impassively as the jury found him guilty of 13 murders and seven attempted murders.

Mr Justice Boreham sentenced him to life imprisonment on each count, adding: 'I shall recommend to the Home Secretary that the minimum period which should elapse before he orders your release shall be 30 years. That is a long period, an unusually long period in my judgement, but you, I believe, are an unusually dangerous man. I express the hope that, when I have said life imprisonment, it will mean precisely that.'

Sutcliffe is currently serving that sentence in the maximum security wing of Parkhurst Prison on the Isle of Wight.

The cruel hoaxer who threw the whole Ripper hunt awry with his mocking Geordie voice – and so helped kill three woman – remains free.

The Lethal Romeo

GEORGE SMITH

Many men have made a living by playing with the affections of plain, naive, lovelorn spinsters, then abandoning them once they have handed over their savings. The public often find the foolish victims of such romantic con-men comic rather than tragic figures, and found reasons for amusement even at the trial of Henri Landru, who was accused of killing ten such dupes. But nobody found anything remotely funny about the exploits of another wicked womaniser, George Joseph Smith.

Smith was born in London's Bethnal Green in 1872, and was soon the despair of his parents. His mother predicted he would 'die with his boots on', and she was hardly surprised when, at the age of only nine, he was sentenced to eight years in a Gravesend reformatory. But the sentence merely helped train him for a life of crime, and, apart from three years as a soldier in the Northamptonshire Regiment, he became a full-time thief, constantly in and out of prison.

Smith was cunning. He realized he was having little success stealing for himself, so he decided to get others to do it for him. Though his bony face was not really attractive, he had small, dark mesmerising eyes that seemed to have an extraordinarily magnetic power for some women. 'They were little eyes that seemed to rob you of your will,' one of his victims told police later.

Smith found it easy to persuade women to work with him, and not to implicate him if they were caught. Using the proceeds of one woman's raids, he opened a baker's shop in Russell Square, Leicester, in 1897, and a year later married an 18-year-old bootmaker's daughter, Caroline Beatrice Thornhill, despite her family's disapproval. He was then 26 and calling himself George Love.

They moved to London, and Smith found his wife employment as a servant with a succession of wealthy families in Brighton, Hove and Hastings. She had no trouble getting work. She had impeccable references from a past employer – Smith. But late in 1899 she was arrested trying to pawn the loot from one theft, some silver spoons, and was jailed for a year. Smith abandoned her, which increased her bitterness, and after her release, she spotted him by chance in London, and alerted the police. In January 1901, he was jailed for two years for receiving stolen goods. Revenge was in his mind, too, once the sentence ended. He travelled to Leicester, bent on killing his wife. But her family beat him up, and Caroline later emigrated to safety in Canada.

Smith had already discovered a new way of making women work for his living. In 1899 he had bigamously married a middle-aged boarding-house keeper, milking her of what money she had while living rent free at her lodgings. Now he began to tour the south coast, particularly seaside resorts, wooing, wedding and walking out on his brides, who were often too humiliated to reveal the truth to police or their friends and relations.

He did it all in the cheapest way possible – third-class rail travel, meagre lodgings, outings to places of free entertainment. In that way, he made the maximum of profit from each of them. In June 1908 he met Florence Wilson, a Worthing widow with £30 in her Post Office savings account. They married in London after a whirlwind three-week affair. On 3 July, he took her to the White City exhibition and left her there, claiming he was going out to buy a newspaper. In fact he dashed back to their rooms in Camden Town and sold all her belongings.

In October 1909, calling himself George Rose, Smith married Southampton spinster Sarah Freeman and they set up home in Clapham, South London. Smith played the charming gent, in smart frock coat and top hat, and his bride did not demur when he said he needed money to set up an antiques business. She withdrew her savings, and sold her Government stocks. On 5 November he took her to the National Gallery, excused himself to go to the lavatory, and scuttled back to their rooms, clearing out everything, and leaving his deserted bride destitute. In less than a month he had made £400, four times the average annual wage.

In between these two coups, Smith had taken another wife, Edith Mabel Pegler. Dark-haired, round-faced and plump, she was 28 when she answered his advertisement for a housekeeper in a local newspaper at Bristol, where he had opened a shop in Gloucester Road. But for once Smith, who used his own name this time, was not after money. What he took from others, he gave to Edith. And though he left her from time to time, claiming he was travelling in search of antiques, he always returned after his matrimonial adventures.

Those adventures now took a more sinister turn. In August 1910, he met 33-year-old spinster Beatrice Constance Anne Mundy while strolling in Clifton, a resort near Bristol. The ardent wooer could hardly believe his luck when she told him of the £2,500 in securities her father, a Wiltshire bank manager, had left her when he died. The legacy, managed by a trust of relatives, paid her £8 a month. Smith, now going under the name of Henry Williams, whisked her off to Weymouth, where they set up home in Rodwell Avenue. They married on 26 August and began to flood the relatives with reassuring letters.

But the relatives had more sense than bride Bessie. They did not like the look of Williams, suspecting that he was a fortune hunter, and it was December before they finally sent £134 owed in interest. Smith, despairing of collecting

George Smith and Beatrice Mundy

> Gangster, racketeer and murderer Al Capone did not die with a
> bullet in his back. He died an ungentlemanly death of
> neurosyphilis. The man whose Twenties crime empire brought in
> $5 million a year and left 1,000 bodies on the streets of Chicago
> died in Florida in 1947, an ex-jailbird with hardly a dime in his
> pocket.

the capital, abandoned Bessie on 13 December in an especially heartless way.
He left her a letter claiming she had 'blighted all my bright hopes of a happy
future' by infecting him with venereal disease, and accusing her of not being
'morally clean.' He was off to London to be cured, 'which will cost me a great
deal of money.' So he took the £134, advising her to tell her relatives it was
stolen while she was asleep on the beach.

Poor Bessie resumed her spinster life, telling friends, on Smith's advice, that
her husband had gone to France. Smith went back to Edith Pegler, moving to
Southend, then London, and back to Bristol again. The VD accusation had
only been an excuse, though it must have upset a woman who was far from
worldly-wise.

That she missed her adoring husband was only too clear when, 18 months
later, they met again by sheer chance in Weston-super-Mare. Bessie, staying
with a friend, popped out to buy daffodils one morning in March 1912, and
spotted Smith on the seafront. The smooth-talking Casanova had an explanation for his note, his long absence, and the fact that he had spent all her
money, and by mid-afternoon the besotted girl was ready to ignore her friend's
pleas and leave with her husband, taking none of her belongings.

They travelled across country, and in May set up a modest home at 80 High
Street, Herne Bay, Kent. Smith had been asking expert advice on how he could
get at Bessie's £2,500 nest-egg, and in July a lawyer told him that it was only
possible if she left it to him in her will. The wily bigamist wasted no time – and
seemingly had no qualms about turning to murder to feather his nest. On 8 July
the couple signed wills, leaving their wordly possessions to each other should
they die. On 9 July, Smith bought a tapless zinc bath, haggling 12½p (half-a-
crown) off the ironmonger's price of £2.

On 10 July, he took Bessie to a young, inexperienced doctor, claiming she had
had a fit. Two days later the doctor called at their home after another fit was
reported. He found Bessie in bed, flushed but seemingly well, and left a
prescription for sedatives. That night, Bessie wrote to her uncle, telling him of
her attacks, of how her husband was looking after her well, and of how they had
both made their wills.

At o8.oo next morning, Saturday 13 July, the doctor received a note saying: 'Can you come at once? I am afraid my wife is dead.' He arrived to find Bessie submerged in the bath. She was naked and lying on her back, a bar of soap clasped in her right hand. Smith said his wife had filled the bath herself, making 20 trips downstairs to the kitchen to fetch water for it. He had gone out to buy some fish, and returned to find her dead. The police were called, but saw no reason to think the death was suspicious. Smith wept throughout the inquest on the following Monday, and was offered words of comfort by the coroner, who recorded a verdict of misadventure.

No-one asked why Bessie had drowned in a bath far shorter than her full height, or why Smith had left her lying under the water until the doctor arrived, instead of trying to resuscitate her. Nor was it found suspicious that she had just made a will, a point Smith was foolish enough to mention to the estate agent when he cancelled the letting of their home.

He had been careful to time the murder for a Saturday. Although he wired news of the death to Bessie's uncle, saying a letter would follow, there was no time for relatives to get to the inquest, or the economy-version funeral which followed just 24 hours later. Trustees of Bessie's legacy asked in vain for a post-mortem examination, and tried to stop Smith getting her money. But he had been too clever for them, and reluctantly they handed over £2,591 13s 6d.

Smith had one last piece of business to attend to. He took the bath back to the ironmonger to avoid having to pay for it. Then he left for Margate, and summoned Edith Pegler to join him. He told her he had made a nice profit selling antiques in Canada, but lost his temper when she revealed that she had been looking for him in Woolwich and Ramsgate. 'He said he did not believe in women knowing his business,' she was to recall. 'He remarked that if I interfered I should never have another happy day.'

Smith was one of the few big-time bigamists not to squander his earnings. He bought eight houses in Bristol with Bessie's money and opened a shop, and also invested in an annuity for himself. By October 1913, he was anxious for more cash, and there seemed no reason why a once-successful scheme should not work again.

Alice Burnham was short, plump and 25, a private nurse to an elderly invalid, when she met a tall, charming stranger at Southsea. Her father, a Buckinghamshire fruit-grower, took an instant dislike to the man, but that did

---

Dr Edward William Pritchard was the last person to be publicly hanged in Scotland. He had murdered his wife and mother-in-law by poisoning them with antimony. No fewer than 100,000 people watched the doctor go to his death in 1865.

not stop her marrying him at Portsmouth on 4 November, one day after he took out a £500 insurance policy on her life. Nor did it stop Smith writing immediately to her father, demanding £104 he was holding for his daughter, and withdrawing £27 from his bride's savings account.

Then he decided to take his new wife on holiday. It was Wednesday, 10 December when they arrived in breezy Blackpool for their bracing, out-of-season break. They called first at a boarding house in Adelaide Street, but Smith rejected the offered rooms – there was no bath. Mrs Crossley at 16 Regent Road had one, however, and the couple booked in there for ten shillings a week. A local doctor was consulted about Mrs Smith's headaches, and the dutiful wife wrote to her father, saying she had 'the best husband in the world.'

On the Friday evening, the couple asked for a bath to be prepared for Mrs Smith while they went for a walk. At 20.15 the Crossleys were having a meal downstairs when they noticed water staining the ceiling. They were about to investigate when a dishevelled Smith appeared at the door carrying two eggs which he said he had just bought for next day's breakfast. Then he went upstairs, and shouted down: 'Fetch the doctor, my wife cannot speak to me.'

Alice had gone the same way as Bessie, and though Smith was asked at the inquest next day why he had not lifted her from the bath, or pulled the plug out of it, an accidental death verdict was recorded. Again Smith wept copiously throughout the hearing, but at least one person was not impressed by his tears. Mrs Crossley was so appalled at his seeming indifference to his wife's death that she refused to let him sleep in her house that Friday night. She also noted that, while waiting for the inquest on the Saturday afternoon, he played the piano in her front room and drank a bottle of whisky.

Even worse was to come. Smith refused to have an expensive coffin for the burial, which took place at noon on Monday. He said: 'When they are dead, they are done with.' He left by train for Southsea – to clear out and sell all Alice's belongings – immediately after the funeral, and Mrs Crossley shouted 'Crippen' at him as he left the house. She also wrote on the address card he gave her: 'Wife died in bath. We shall see him again.' She could not know how prophetic those words were.

Smith rejoined the faithful Edith Pegler at Bristol in time for Christmas and used the £500 insurance money to increase his annuity. By August they were in Bournemouth, via London Cheltenham and Torquay. Smith announced he was going up to London again, alone, for a few days. He had met and wooed a maid called Alice Reavil while listening to a band on the seafront. They married at Woolwich on 17 September, but Smith did not stay long. He was back in Bristol with the girl's £80 savings and some of her clothes – a gift for Edith – by late autumn.

The callous truth was that Alice was so poor she was not worth killing. Smith

THE LETHAL ROMEO

Blood-shedding Mongol leader Genghis Khan never let up on his bouts of mayhem and murder – even when he was in his coffin. He left orders that if anyone looked at his coffin, his funeral guards were to ensure that the next coffin would be theirs.

Genghis Khan once had 70 enemy chiefs stewed alive. He did not believe in taking prisoners and tore open victims' bellies in case they were hiding jewels. His prisoners' heads would be cut and banked up in sickly pyramids.

Genghis Khan is reputed to have been the biggest mass killer in history. He is believed to have been responsible for the deaths of 20 million people – one-tenth of the world's population at that time. He died in 1227.

abandoned her in some public gardens after a long tram ride. But he already had a third murder victim in mind. He had met Miss Margaret Lofty, a 38-year-old clergyman's daughter, in Bath the previous June. She worked as a lady's companion, living between jobs with her elderly widowed mother. And she was ripe for exploitation – she had discovered earlier in the year that her 'fiance' was a married man.

Smith was now calling himself John Lloyd and posing as an estate agent. He took her out to tea on 15 December and two days later they were married in secret. Smith had taken the precaution of persuading his beloved to insure her life for £700 and had even generously paid the first premium. They moved to London, taking rooms at 14 Bismarck Road, Highgate. Naturally they had a bath. But Smith seemed to have grown over-confident after the success of his two previous killings. This time he was amazingly impatient.

He took Margaret to see a local doctor on their evening of arrival, 17 December. Next morning, he took her to a solicitor to make her will – leaving everything to him. Then she wrote to her mother, describing her husband as 'a thorough Christian man.' By 20.00 on 18 December, she was having a bath. Her landlady, ironing downstairs, later recalled a splashing sound, and a noise 'as of someone putting wet hands or arms on the side of the bath.' Then there was a sigh, followed by the strains of the hymn Nearer My Go To Thee on the harmonium in the front room. Ten minutes later the landlady answered the doorbell and found 'Mr Lloyd' standing outside, saying he had forgotten his key after popping out to buy tomatoes for his wife's supper. Sadly, Mrs Lloyd was not alive to eat them.

Though Margaret was buried on the following Monday morning, the inquest was held over until after Christmas. Smith hurried home to Bristol again, and even had the cheek to tell Edith to beware of taking a bath, adding:

'It is known that women have often lost their lives through weak hearts and fainting in the bath.' That had been the coroner's verdict on Alice Burnham, and the Highgate coroner saw no reason to think differently when he considered the death of Margaret 'Lloyd' on 1 January, 1915.

But it was to be no happy new year for George Joseph Smith. His impatience to get rid of Margaret proved his undoing. The previous deaths had not attracted too much press attention. But this one had all the ingredients of a front page story. 'Found dead in bath,' said the headline in the *News Of The World*. A second headline read: 'Bride's Tragic Fate On Day After Wedding.'

Two readers, miles apart, noticed the story and thought it was too much of a coincidence. In Buckinghamshire, Alice Burnham's father contacted his solicitor, who went to the police. And in Blackpool, landlady Mrs Crossley also passed on her fears to the authorities. They began investigating possible connections between John Lloyd, estate agent, and George Smith, bachelor of independent means, and pieced together the incredible story of Smith's bigamous philanderings. On 1 February, a detective inspector and two sergeants arrested the deadly bridegroom as he left his solicitor's office, where he was making arrangements to collect the £700 insurance on his third victim.

Though the bodies of all three women were exhumed, and examined by famous pathologist Sir Bernard Spilsbury, there were no obvious signs of how they had drowned. And though Smith was charged with all three murders, he could only be tried, under English law, with one, that of Bessie Mundy. Smith denied strenuously that he had murdered anyone. He described the deaths of three brides in the same way as a 'phenomenal coincidence.' Any jury might have been prepared to accept that one such death was just an unfortunate accident. The prosecution therefore had to apply for permission to produce evidence about all three killings to show proof of a 'system.' Smith's attorney, Sir Edward Marshall Hall, protested, realizing that his only hope of a successful defence would be destroyed. But Mr Justice Scrutton agreed to consider all three deaths.

Marshall Hall, who believed privately that Smith used hypnotic powers to persuade all three wives to kill themselves, had another setback before the trial. Some newspapers had agreed to foot the defence bill in return for Smith's

---

In 1880, at the age of 26, Australian bushranger Ned Kelly was hanged at the end of a rope, watched by a huge crowd outside Melbourne jail. Kelly and his gang had killed at least four troopers in their flight from the law. Ned Kelly's last words on the scaffold were: 'Such is life!'

exclusive life story. But the Home Office vetoed the plan, and since all Smith's money was tied up in annuities, Marshall Hall received only a paltry fee under the Poor Persons Defence Act.

He received no help at all from his client. Smith repeatedly soured opinions, both at committals and at his trial, which began at the Old Bailey on 22 June, 1915, with bad-tempered outbursts at witnesses, his own lawyers and the judge. At one stage he screamed: 'It's a disgrace to a Christian country, this is. I'm not a murderer, though I may be a bit peculiar.'

The irony of the timing of the trial during World War One was not lost on Mr Justice Scrutton. A month before it, 1,198 lives were lost when a German submarine torpedoed the *Lusitania*. On the morning the trial began, *The Times* listed 3,100 men killed in the trenches. 'And yet,' said the judge in his summing-up, 'while this wholesale destruction of human life is going on, for some days all the apparatus of justice in England has been considering whether the prosecution are right in saying that one man should die.'

It took the jury only 22 minutes on 1 July to decide that he should. They had heard pathologist Spilsbury explain how Smith could have lifted his brides' legs with his left arm while pushing their heads under water with his right. And they had watched a dramatic reconstruction of such a possibility, carried out by a detective and a nurse in a bathing costume in an ante-room of the court. Even though the nurse knew what was about to happen, she still needed artificial respiration after her ordeal.

Smith was taken from Pentonville Jail to Maidstone Prison, still protesting his innocence. He remained unrepentant, though he turned to religion and was confirmed by the Bishop of Croydon, who was said to be impressed with his sincerity. On the eve of his execution, Smith wrote to Edith Pegler, who had wept for him outside the Old Bailey, saying: 'May an old age, serene and bright, and as lovely as a Lapland night, lead thee to thy grave. Now, my true love, goodbye until we meet again.'

Edith alone mourned on Friday, 13 August, when Smith was led to his execution. One day later, his first and only legal wife, Caroline Thornhill, took advantage of her widowhood to marry a Canadian soldier in Leicester.

Atlanta's Streets of Fear

WAYNE WILLIAMS

The 'Missing and Murdered Children' file in the Atlanta Police headquarters had 26 unsolved cases by late spring of 1981. Throughout the two previous years black children had been snatched from the streets or simply disappeared in this town in America's deep south and it was sometimes months before their bodies were discovered hidden in undergrowth or dumped in a river. Murder had reached epidemic proportions in Atlanta. The victims were always coloured and often too young to have had any chance to defend themselves. Death was usually due to strangulation. Forensic experts believed the children, one of whom was aged only seven, were being attacked from behind by a man who squeezed the life out of them by locking his arm around their necks.

A shroud of fear fell over the town while the homicidal maniac stalked the streets. At night the roads and the pavements were deserted. Parents too scared to let their children out of their sight for more than a few seconds were locking their doors to keep them inside. Vigilante parent patrols were formed. Fathers often armed themselves with baseball bats.. And over everything hung suspicion. Was a white man carrying out his own macabre mission against blacks or was a crazy cult killer on the loose?

The two-year search for the killer had broken the health of many senior police officers, stretched the resources of the whole town and even caused the State Justice Department to set up a special unit to join in the hunt. Every time another child went missing the efforts were intensified. But despite millions of dollars spent, the murders continued.

FBI officers had to be drafted in to Atlanta to help police chief Lee Brown who was under universal attack from the townspeople. And hordes of cranks arrived in town eager to pick up the $100,000 reward for information leading to the arrest of the killer. It was a frightening and macabre mystery – made the worse by the fact that the police believed the killer was taunting them.

After November 1980, when the eleventh killing occurred, children were being murdered at intervals of about three and a half weeks. The bodies, instead of being hidden, were left conspicuously in parks. And despite all precautions the parents were taking, the killer was still finding victims.

As he stepped up his campaign of death, a grisly pattern was beginning to

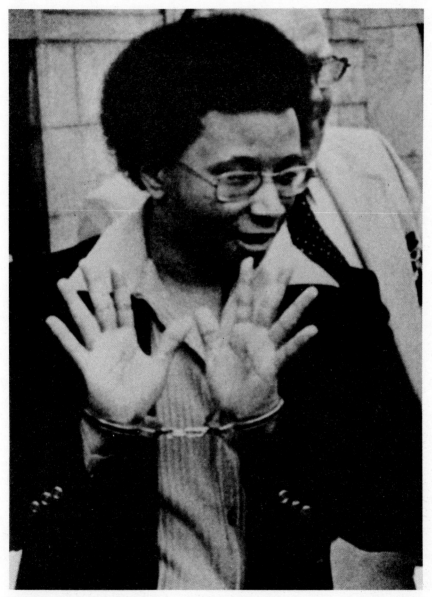

Wayne Williams leaving Fulton County Court, August 1981

emerge. All the children had been aged between 7 and 14 years and all but two were boys. Yet despite fears of a crazed pervert being on the loose, there was no evidence that any of the children had been sexually assaulted. Worse, the police were worried that if just one person was responsible for all the deaths then other psychopaths may be encouraged by the apparent ease and lack of detection. The desperate hunt for the killer was one of the biggest police operations ever launched in the United States. Twenty-thousand citizens were interviewed by officers, another 150,000 were questioned over the telephone. Tens of thousands of children were spoken to because the police believed that at sometime the killer could have tried to abduct a child unsuccessfully. Thirty-five FBI agents were permanently stationed in Atlanta and had been told they would stay there until the investigation was over.

Then one night in May 1981 there was a dramatic breakthrough. Two police officers and two FBI agents were huddled in a corner under the arches of the four-lane South Drive Bridge. They were one of dozens of teams which undertook around-the-clock vigils in the city. Ironically they were not watching the river on that misty night. They were merely covering the bridge because it formed one of the main routes to and from the town and they could quickly be on the road to join in any chase or stop any suspect leaving Atlanta. But as they chatted in whispers they were startled by something splashing into the water only a metre or so away. Two of the men went into the water to try to help whoever had gone in, and two sprinted up to the road and were there within a few seconds. They radioed ahead and a patrol car arrived almost instantly at the end of the bridge and stopped the traffic coming off it. Drivers were questioned briefly and then allowed to go on their ways.

Two days later police frogmen fished out of the river the body of Nathaniel Cater a 27-year-old negro. Strangulation was given as the cause of death.

If the same killer had struck again, then he had broken his pattern. The victim was black and had died from strangulation . . . but he was an adult. There

---

John Lee was the man they could not hang. Lee, a 19-year-old servant with a previous conviction for theft, was controversially found guilty of murdering his employer, Miss Emma Keyse, who had her throat cut and skull crushed in November 1884. Three times, he took his place on the scaffold, but each time the trapdoor refused to open, though it worked perfectly when tested with weights in between. Lee, who said: 'It was the Lord's hand which would not let the law take away my life,' was given a prison sentence instead, and released in 1907 after serving 22 years. He then married, emigrated to America, and died there in 1933.

Anna Maria Zwanziger took a terrible revenge on the legal profession after her husband, an alcoholic lawyer, died leaving her only debts. She took housekeeping jobs in the homes of judges, then proceeded to poison her employers and their families.

She is known to have murdered one judge who refused to marry her, the wives of two more, and the child of one of them. Altogether, she poisoned an estimated 80 people, though most escaped with violent illness. After her arrest, police noticed that she trembled with pleasure when confronted with arsenic powder. She was executed by the sword in Bavaria in 1811.

---

were enough similarities for the police to suspect that Cater was number 27 in the chain of killings. The 'Missing and Murdered Children' file was renamed 'Missing and Murdered People'.

A few days later the body of a second victim, 21-year-old Ray Payne, also a negro, was recovered from the river. He had been thrown in at the same time as Cater and had also died from strangulation. Knowing that four of the child victims had previously been recovered from the river, the investigation team went back to the drivers they had stopped on the night the surveillance team had been under the bridge.

One of the men they questioned was Wayne Bertram Williams a 23-year-old black who lived quietly with his parents, both retired school-teachers, in a modest single-storey house in north-west Atlanta. He was taken to the city police headquarters and held overnight but was released despite the police discovery that he lived a bizarre lifestyle and considered himself a genius. Williams was a self-described 'media groupie'. He used to sit around in his car with a short-wave radio and tune in to police and fire services listening out for crimes or fires. Then, equipped with a camera, he would rush to the scene, usually arriving ahead of reporters and television crews and sell his exclusive pictures to the highest bidder. At the age of 14 he had started broadcasting on his own small pirate radio station in Atlanta. An only and lonely child, he had been convicted at 18 of impersonating a police officer. All his friends were shocked and surprised when they learnt that he was a police suspect.

On 3 June he was again taken in for questioning by police and given a 12-hour grilling. The next day, he rang newspapers and TV stations and held a press conference. Professing his innocence, he claimed the police had told him he was the prime suspect in some of the slayings. He said: 'One cop told me "You killed Nathaniel Cater. It's just a matter of time before we get you." I never killed anybody and I never threw anything from the bridge.'

For the next two and a half weeks Williams was under constant surveillance.

THE WORLD'S MOST INFAMOUS MURDERS

Charles Whitman went to pieces after his parents split up in March 1966. The 25-year-old student complained of headaches, showed violent temper tantrums, and became convinced he had a growth in his brain which was making him mentally ill. In the early hours of 1 August, he stabbed and shot his mother, then stabbed his wife. Taking several pistols, a radio and sandwiches, he climbed a 100 metres high observation tower at the University of Texas in Austin, clubbing a receptionist to death and barricading the stairway.

Two people climbing to the tower were shot, and at 11.40, Whitman, an expert shot after Marine service, began shooting indiscriminately at students. He killed 16 and wounded 30 in the next 90 minutes, defying attempts by police and low-flying aircraft to dislodge him. Finally police stormed the barricade he had built, and shot him to pieces. They later found a note from him saying: 'Life is not worth living.'

And then the results of tests on fibres taken from his car came from the laboratory. The fibres matched those on clothing of murder victims Cater and Payne. Williams was arrested and indicted on the charge of murdering Cater. The Payne charge was added later.

The police then faced up to the real problem of trying to get Williams convicted. Their evidence was not good. They had no witnesses either to the killings or the dumping of the bodies. All their hopes were pinned on the wizardry of the forensic scientists.

Their fears were justified as the nine-week trial got under way. Firstly, there was no motive, though prosecution lawyers suggested that Williams was 'a frustrated man driven by a desire to purify the black race by murdering poor young blacks'. Defending the accused man was Alvin Binder a well-known Mississippi trial lawyer, who was clearly scoring points as he tore the prosecution's evidence into shreds. Then the trial took a remarkable turn when the judge made a surprise ruling after a plea from the prosecution. With their case literally hanging by threads, the lawyers persuaded him to allow them to introduce evidence linking Williams to the deaths of ten other victims. The assistant District Attorney, Joseph Drolet, said: 'He has not been formally charged with the killings but the cases will reveal a pattern and bent of mind.'

The evidence brought to life a case that had slipped into a repetition of complicated forensic evidence. A boy aged 15 said he had been fondled by Williams who he later saw with 14-year-old Lubie Geter whose decomposed body was found clad only in underpants. Other witnesses said they had spotted him with more of the victims. One music business contact of Williams' said the accused man had once passed him a note which said: 'I could be a mayor – I could even be a killer.'

When Williams took the stand he denied everything. No, he had not stopped his car on the bridge, nor even slowed down. No, he had not thrown Cater's body over nor did he believe he would have had the strength to lift it. No, he was not a homosexual. Yes, all the witnesses and even the police had lied. He told the jury: 'I never met any of the victims. I feel just as sorry for them as anybody else in the world. I am 23 years old and I could have been one of the people killed out there.'

Later, under persistent cross-examination, he accused the prosecutor of being a fool and he described two FBI men who had interviewed him as 'goons'.

Finally the jury of eight blacks and four whites retired. They deliberated for 12 hours before returning a verdict of 'Guilty'.

As he was being led away to start two consecutive life terms Williams turned with tears streaming down his face, and protested his innocence 'from my heart'. His father, Homer Williams, cried out: 'It's impossible to find a young man like this guilty.' But guilty he was found and he went to jail knowing that it would be 14 years before he could be eligible for parole.

His lawyers immediately made plans to appeal – a process which many expected to take years.

The Case of the Lethal 'Cuppa'

GRAHAM YOUNG

He was the most charming and efficient tea boy. His coffee was good, too. But a price had to be paid for it. It cost two people their lives. In April 1971, 23-year-old Londoner Graham Young, who was on a government training course at Slough, Berkshire, answered a 'help wanted' advertisment in a local paper. It said that John Hadland, manufacturers of specialist, highspeed optical and photographic instruments, needed a storeman at their small factory in the Hertfordshire village of Bovingdon.

Young said on his application form that he had 'previously studied chemistry, organic and inorganic, pharmacology and toxicology over the past 10 years' and had 'some knowledge of chemicals'.

He told the managing director, Mr Godfrey Foster, that before going to the training centre he had a nervous breakdown after his mother's death and had had mental treatment. Mr Foster was sent the report of a psychiatrist who had treated Young. It said that Young had made 'an extremely full recovery' from a 'deep-going personality disorder' and would 'do extremely well training as a storekeeper'. It also said Young was of above-average intelligence and 'would fit in well and not draw any attention to himself in any community'.

The report was hopelessly wrong on all counts – as Young's workmates were to find out. They did their best to make him feel at home, and he was befriended in particular by the head storeman, Bob Egle, 59, Frederick Biggs, 61, head of the works-in-progress department, and storeman-driver Ronald Hewitt, 41. Rob and Frederick would often lend him cigarettes and money, and Young offered to get tea and coffee for everybody who was kind to him.

Then a strange illness which was nicknamed the 'Bovingdon Bug' began to hit the staff at Hadland's. About 70 members of the staff went down with the illness. Symptoms included diarrhoea, stomach pains, loss of hair and numbness in the legs. Some said their tea tasted bitter, and a medical team was called in to find out if the chemicals used at the factory were responsible. The 'bug' killed two members of the staff – the kindly Bob Egle and Frederick Biggs. Bob died first. He became ill less than a month after Young joined the firm. His condition deteriorated rapidly and he was admitted to hospital. His heart

THE CASE OF THE LETHAL 'CUPPA'

Above: Broadmore where Young was sent as a 14-year-old schoolboy

Left: Graham Young, aged 24

stopped twice while he was in intensive care unit and he died, paralyzed, on 7 July. Young appeared to be very concerned at Egle's death and attended the funeral. Then, in September 1972, Frederick was taken ill with stomach pains and vomiting. He died three weeks later in a London hospital.

When he heard about it Young is reported to have said: 'Poor old Fred. I wonder what went wrong? He shouldn't have died. I was very fond of old Fred.'

With Biggs' death, panic set in at the factory and several employees threatened to resign. Iain Anderson, the firm's medical officer, became suspicious when Young boasted about his knowledge of medicine and poisons. Detective Chief Inspector John Kirkland, of Hemel Hempstead police, was called in and asked Scotland Yard to check Young's background. When the answer came back, Young was arrested on suspicion of murder.

Police found that his bedsitter was full of bottles containing various chemicals and poisons, and the walls plastered with photographs of his heroes – Hitler and other Nazi leaders. A bottle of thallium, a deadly poison, tasteless and odourless, was found on Young when he was arrested.

Young went on trial at St Albans in July 1972. It took the jury less than an hour to find him guilty of two murders, two attempted murders and two charges of administering poison.

He was jailed for life and placed in a top security hospital. But it was only there that his background came to light. The hospital in which he had been treated for his breakdown turned out to be Broadmoor. In 1962 he had pleaded guilty at the Old Bailey to poisoning his father, his sister and a friend. Young was, in fact, a compulsive poisoner before he was 15.

Mr Justice Melford Stevenson had committed Young to Broadmoor with a recommendation that he should not be released for 15 years. He was discharged nine years later as having made 'an extremely full recovery', and the result was that two kindly innocent men died.

PDO 83-229